STUDIES IN FRENCH LITERATURE No. 16

*General Editor*
W. G. Moore
Fellow and Tutor of St. John's College, Oxford

# GEORGES BERNANOS:
# JOURNAL D'UN
# CURÉ DE CAMPAGNE

by

## J. E. FLOWER

*Lecturer in French in the School of European Studies,*
*University of East Anglia*

EDWARD ARNOLD

First published 1970 by
Edward Arnold (Publishers) Ltd.,
41 Maddox Street, London, W.1.

Paper edition SBN: 7131 5539 6
Cloth edition SBN: 7131 5538 8

*Printed in Great Britain by*
*The Camelot Press Ltd.,*
*London and Southampton*

# Contents

# Acknowledgments

The editor and publishers wish to thank the following for their permission to reproduce copyright material: Librairie Plon for extracts from the *Journal d'un curé de campagne*, and Editions Gallimard for short extracts from *Monsieur Ouine*; Editions du Seuil for short extracts from *Bernanos par lui-même*, by Albert Béguin.

*J'écris chacun de mes livres pour me confirmer dans le sentiment que j'ai de la vie. Ma foi est incorporée aujourd'hui à l'univers, tel que je le connais, tel que je le vois.*

GEORGES BERNANOS

# Foreword

Criticism of Bernanos' work to date has been almost entirely thematic in its approach. In other words critics have selected one of the predominant motifs of his writing—sainthood, poverty, love or the spirit of childhood for example—illustrating it copiously, and with varying degrees of success, from as wide a selection of texts as possible. This has resulted in a series of books many of which are little more than fuller but frequently no better versions of Albert Béguin's admirable *Bernanos par lui-même*,[1] and what exceptions there are can only be considered such on account of the depth of their analyses or the length and clarity of their exposition.[2] It is of course possible to argue that such a method is both valid and necessary for the study of any writer whose private convictions and public statements were so inextricably mixed together and so passionately held that they charged everything he wrote and even on occasions caused his pen to run away with him to the detriment of his argument or narrative. As far as his novels are concerned, however, it is also true that very little work has been done to examine their standing as pieces of imaginative literature rather than as vehicles for certain ideas. *Monsieur Ouine* has been exhaustively studied by Professor Bush particularly in his book *Angoisse du mystère*,[3] but his concern has been above all for the apparent fragmentary nature of the novel, and for the most part his aim has been to present us with a definitive solution to the textual confusion which has surrounded *Monsieur Ouine* rather than with an analysis of the many problems of interpretation which it raises.

Of all the novels the *Journal d'un curé de campagne* has to date claimed the most consistent and closest attention: in particular it has been the subject of the second volume of the *Etudes bernanosiennes*, has appeared in the form of an *édition scolaire* both in this country and in France, and has been studied in a number of articles and individual chapters of general books on Bernanos. Yet there is still room and need for further detailed work both on this and other individual novels, as well as on the much

[1] Paris, 1954. Details of this and other studies considered to be particularly useful are to be found in the Bibliography, pp. 63,4.

[2] See in particular the studies by Balthasar, Estève and Milner.

[3] Minard, Paris, 1967.

greater issue of evaluating Bernanos' achievements as a novelist in the light of his various statements concerning the problems of novel writing, and in particular those which face him as a Catholic. Largely on account of the series' requirements, the commentary in Michel Estève's Livre de Poche edition is brief, while most of his critical points are to be found in his notes to the Pléiade edition of Bernanos' *Œuvres romanesques* and in an article for *Le Français dans le monde*.[4] Both he and Dr. O'Sharkey (in her English edition) have missed an opportunity for coming to grips with the book itself, for examining the structure and tensions that underlie it and which are largely responsible for its being regarded by the majority of Bernanos' critics as his masterpiece. This is not to say that their work is without value; far from it. Indeed with her edition Dr. O'Sharkey has provided a useful addition to Peter Hebblethwaite's book which had hitherto stood as the only major contribution to Bernanos studies in English. It is the aim of this essay, however, to add to the work of these critics by examining in particular the way in which Bernanos has sought to create the most appropriate vehicle for his ideas. The *Journal d'un curé de campagne* is one of the most complex books to have been written during the first half of this century, and I can only hope that in attempting to analyse its principal features I have not over-simplified them.

4 Details of these editions and articles are given on p. 63. All page references in this book are to the Plon edition of the novel published in 1936.

# 1. Introduction

Having contended that the thematic approach adopted by many of Bernanos' critics is not necessarily the correct one, it is nonetheless useful to outline the principal elements of his thinking if we are to appreciate the skill with which he has embodied them in his novels and in the *Journal d'un curé de campagne* in particular. Of all his personal characteristics those which seem to have struck his contemporaries most forcibly are his energy, enthusiasm and readiness to defend what he believed in to his utmost. That this was so even from an early age is suggested by his academic success both at school and at university, and by his political activities before the first World War as one of the *camelots du roi*, the young, often violent supporters of Charles Maurras' monarchist movement, the Action Française. Even letters written during the early years of the century to his friend the abbé Lagrange show how both his style and his thinking were influenced by Maurras' unyielding dogmatism:

> Je resterai dogmatique en diable, dégoûté des compromissions d'idées et de reculades de principes, absolument persuadé que le sort de la France—même au point de vue religieux—dépend d'une politique traditionnelle positive, de faits précis et concrétisés, qui est, à tout le moins, la seule accommodée au tempérament national et à la race, puisque c'est la race qui l'a faite.[1]

Such vigour and forcefulness were to characterize him in all he did or said throughout his life. Indeed when Richard Griffiths, writing of Bernanos' political affiliations at the time of the Spanish Civil War, remarks that 'he had in a certain sense, changed sides; but his opinions were essentially the same',[2] the statement is not so paradoxical as it may at first appear. Bernanos may have 'changed sides' as far as much of the outside world was concerned, but essentially he was being consistent in his hatred of oppression and totalitarianism, and in his bitterness for all forms of cowardice and compromise particularly where the Catholic Church was involved. So sickened was he eventually by what he termed

[1] *Œuvres romanesques*, p. 1736.
[2] Richard Griffiths, *The Reactionary Revolution*, Constable, London, 1966, p. 358.

the 'mediocrity' of contemporary France that he deliberately exiled himself to Brazil until De Gaulle magisterially recalled him in 1945 with the words 'Votre place est parmi nous'.

At the root of all Bernanos' political and social attitudes lies his religious faith without which, as he recognized as early as 1905, life would be meaningless for him:

> je reconnais plus que jamais que la vie, même avec la gloire, qui est la plus belle chose humaine, est une chose vide et sans saveur quand on n'y mêle pas, toujours, absolument, Dieu.[3]

Unlike Claudel, whose ambition it had been to become a member of the regular clergy, Bernanos argued that as a lay member of the Catholic Church not only were there certain advantages which it was his privilege to enjoy, but that there were areas where he could have at least as much effect as a priest, if not more, by conveying his personal religious convictions through his writing.[4]

It is significant that these references should be to letters written when Bernanos was a young man. Subsequent evidence reveals that his position was hardly modified, his religious and political convictions emerging as the large dominant themes in his literary works, sometimes falsifying them or rendering them unpalatable—as in the second part of *L'Imposture* where he bitterly attacks ineffective social Catholic groups and their aims —but always reminding us that for Bernanos these works were just as important as vehicles for his public statements as articles and the more conventional volumes of journalistic writing.

His first novel, *Sous le soleil de Satan*, written in 1925 at the relatively late age of thirty-seven was, as some contemporary critics saw, and as Bernanos himself confessed, an attempt to revitalize the Catholic faith in a country which was rapidly becoming dechristianized.[5] *Sous le soleil de Satan* is a melodramatic, colourful statement on a grand scale, of a message which Bernanos wishes all his readers to grasp: good and evil in the persons of the abbé Donissan and Satan himself clash as in a medieval morality play, with good ultimately emerging triumphant even at the expense of pain and death. The struggle takes place against a background of the corrupt society that is to become a regular feature of Bernanos' novels, a society where young girls are led astray, where amateur

[3] *Œuvres romanesques*, p. 1727.    [4] *Œuvres romanesques*, p. 1730.
[5] *Le Crépuscule des vieux*, Gallimard, Paris, 1956, p. 11.

politicians and doctors are seen as agents of the Devil, and where members of the clergy willingly look for material comfort instead of girding up their cassocks to fight the apathy and spiritual aridity of their parishioners. And just as Bernanos' ideas remain constant, so too do the images through which he conveys them. Mud and decay herald corruption; an open road or window frequently symbolizes his vision of unending hope for a new eternal Christian society; blue eyes denote purity and innocence, black eyes and outbursts of uncontrollable laughter hint at the presence of the Devil himself.

Society, Bernanos maintains, has become the willing victim of a number of systems—political, social, technological, even religious—all of which have relieved man of the need to think and act independently. Instead what is required is 'cette espèce d'homme que le dix-septième siècle appelait l'honnête homme',[6] by which Bernanos means the man who would only act in accordance with the values dictated to him by his *individual* conscience and prompted by religious faith. In placing such emphasis on this faith, however, Bernanos is not necessarily accepting the interpretation given to it by the Catholic Church now or at any time in the last three hundred years, for it too has become complacent and has sought to avoid crises rather than face up to them. As we might expect, Bernanos believes in action; Christianity must be a living, vital matter which actively wages war on the forces of evil, and to shirk this on the grounds that we are being prudent is tantamount to acknowledging defeat or to giving up the struggle altogether. Even though, like the abbé Donissan, Chevance or the curé d'Ambricourt, we may be physically overcome by the evil that surrounds us, we must be prepared to struggle ceaselessly, for only in this way can we prove the strength and durability of our faith. Evil faces us not as a series of catastrophic events each to be challenged in turn, but as a continuous stifling, choking presence, of which we are made aware by Bernanos' references to the slime and mud in the parish of Fenouille in *Monsieur Ouine*, or the dust and fine rain in the *Journal d'un curé de campagne*. To ignore the problem of evil or to pretend deliberately that it does not exist is, for Bernanos, the most heinous sin of all, and in his denunciation of this attitude we frequently find him employing the epithets *imbéciles* and *médiocres*, not, as some of his journalism might suggest, out of a taste for verbal violence, but because, as

---

[6] Quoted by Balthasar (p. 86) from some notes sent by Bernanos to Fernando Carneiro in 1944.

Balthasar has pointed out, the two words in their original meanings denote weakness and an inability to accept commitment. In adopting such an attitude Bernanos reveals clear affinities with writers and thinkers as different from one another as Pascal and Sartre, both of whom (though for quite different reasons) are contemptuous of those who refuse to face up to the dilemma of their existence. Pascal's *divertissement* and Sartre's *mauvaise foi* are both essentially defence mechanisms which provide people with a short cut to what they believe constitutes security, but the unthinking, automatic behaviour of which these are symptomatic only serves to maintain a state of inertia in which positive, creative choice becomes increasingly difficult. Like Bernanos each of these writers acknowledges man's basic freedom which it is his duty to preserve, though as Christians Pascal and Bernanos believe that freedom can only be fully used if it willingly acknowledges and accepts the ultimate omniscient divine presence. For them such a choice, freely made, guarantees eternal salvation; for Sartre, of course, death nullifies all our actions.[7]

For the most part Bernanos argues that man is in grave danger of misusing his freedom by failing to place his faith in God. It is not, as some of his early critics tried to suggest, that he accepts a simplist Jansenism whereby some souls are already promised to the Devil, nor is he guilty of Manichaeism, the heretical belief which argues that the world is equally shared between the forces of good and evil. For Bernanos, good must ultimately triumph because Satan is allowed a certain limited role only, but by giving man the freedom to choose, God has nonetheless assured the Devil of a number of victims in spite of the expiatory sufferings and sacrifices of all the saints.

At once it becomes obvious that the saints, or saint figures, in Bernanos' work are the very persons who do not allow themselves to be trapped by the Devil's wiles. Yet Bernanos does not endow them with any superhuman qualities; there is nothing heroically glorious in his saints[8] but instead, as Dr. O'Sharkey observes, 'a day-to-day fidelity and the conquest of despair by a supernatural hope'.[9] Or, as another English critic, Dr. Ernest Beaumont, very tellingly states, the Devil must be ignored and overcome 'by a childish simplicity and humility, an utter defenceless-

---

[7] 'Pourquoi dit-on "avancer dans la vie"? C'est dans la mort qu'on avance, c'est notre mort que nous approfondissons, sans cesse, ainsi qu'une œuvre lente à venir.' *Sept*, 5 June, 1936.

[8] *La Liberté, pour quoi faire?*, Gallimard, Paris, 1953, p. 286.

[9] O'Sharkey, Edition, p. 13.

ness'.[10] In no way are they singled out for divine support and, like Christ himself, with whom they clearly have many affinities,[11] they are left to face the temptations of the Devil alone; their strength lies in their faith. Chantal de Clergerie in *La Joie*, Blanche de la Force in the *Dialogue des Carmélites* and the curé d'Ambricourt may, for example, become aware that they differ from other people, even that they are 'prisonniers de la Sainte Agonie', but such realization dawns only late in life. For the most part Bernanos stresses their human qualities and in particular the manner in which they suffer and despair. They are all either frail, undernourished, or suffering from an incurable disease; they are ill at ease in the company of others and frequently incompetent in their duties. Unlike the complacent mediocre priests or the apostate Cénabre, all of whom enjoy material comfort and good health, they live permanently on the edge of poverty.[12] Such discomfort renders them vulnerable to the Devil's approaches and in particular prompts them to doubt the value of their lives and the humility that is required of them. Donissan is characteristically violent in his attempts to convince himself that he is doing his job as a priest for the love of God only; he beats any thought of self-indulgence or pride out of himself with a steel chain lash, and the blood-stained walls of his cell bear witness to the extent to which he tortures himself. The curé d'Ambricourt too is tormented by the Devil, though he refrains from inflicting such physical violence upon himself. All of them, however, resist the ultimate temptation to surrender their souls to the Devil, and it is from the depths of despair when they are at their most vulnerable that they are saved by their unshakable faith and are also marked out from the rest of mankind:

> Chaque homme prédestiné, au moins une fois dans sa vie, a cru couler à pic, toucher le fond. L'illusion que tout nous manque à la fois, ce sentiment de complète dépossession est le signe divin qu'au contraire tout commence.[13]

These essential characteristics which Bernanos stresses in his saints are

---

[10] 'Georges Bernanos, 1888–1948', in *The Novelist as Philosopher* (ed. J. Cruickshank), London, 1962, p. 41.

[11] See in particular a further article by Dr. Beaumont, 'Le sens christique de l'œuvre romanesque de Bernanos', *Etudes bernanosiennes*, No. 3/4, pp. 87–106.

[12] The curé de Torcy is an obvious exception to this. See below, p. 40.

[13] *Saint Dominique*, Gallimard, Paris, 1939, p. 22.

symbolized by his references to them as children.[14] In his small volume on Joan of Arc, *Jeanne relapse et sainte*, we read: 'La plupart [des saints] sont des enfants' and 'Les saints et les héros sont des hommes qui ne sont pas sortis de l'enfance'.[15] Just as a child unswervingly places its trust in its parents, so the saints look to God and to the mother church for guidance and protection.

These, briefly, are the predominant characteristics of Bernanos' thought. He acknowledges the very real presence of evil in the world and believes that passive resistance alone is not sufficient if it is to be overcome. In the last analysis it is through his written work and in particular through his novels that he indicates not only the spiritual aridity of contemporary society but also clear measures for its improvement, and it is to his credit that in doing so he is frequently able to avoid undisguised didacticism. That he was aware of the problems and indeed dangers involved in writing imaginative literature based on subjects of such a metaphysical nature as religious faith, is clear from the Preface to the *Grands cimetières sous la lune*: 'J'écris dans les salles de cafés ainsi que j'écrivais jadis dans les wagons de chemin de fer, pour ne pas être dupe de créatures imaginaires.'[16] In the *Journal d'un curé de campagne*, however, Bernanos' achievement goes beyond his choice of authentic characters and situations. This book in particular shows him writing a work which has much more control than any of his others, with the tensions and balance of his story providing the vehicle for ideas that elsewhere obtrude and provoke the accusation of a *roman à thèse*.

[14] See in particular Bridel's study.

[15] Op. cit., Plon, Paris, 1934, p. 62; *Français, si vous saviez*, Gallimard, Paris, 1961, p. 270.

[16] Op. cit., Livre de poche, p. 7.

# 2. Origins

The *Journal d'un curé de campagne* belongs to that period in Bernanos' life from October 1934 to March 1937 aptly defined by Michel Estève as 'trente mois d'une exceptionnelle fécondité'.[1] Having emigrated to Palma in order, he hoped, to reduce the cost of living for his by now large family, Bernanos was already writing three novels—*Un Mauvais Rêve*, *Un Crime* and *Monsieur Ouine*. During the summer of 1934 he abandoned *Monsieur Ouine* at Chapter sixteen and turned his attention once again to *Un Crime* of which he completed a first version by the end of the year. On discovering, however, that the two parts of the book no longer properly matched one another, it too was put aside and the *Journal d'un curé de campagne* was begun.

One letter in particular, written in January 1935, indicates something of his hopes and intentions:

> J'ai commencé un beau vieux livre, que vous aimerez, je crois. J'ai résolu de faire le journal d'un jeune prêtre, à son entrée dans une paroisse. Il va chercher midi à quatorze heures, se démener comme quatre, faire des projets mirifiques, qui échoueront naturellement, se laisser plus ou moins duper par des imbéciles, des vicieuses ou des salauds, et alors qu'il croira tout perdu, il aura servi le bon Dieu dans la mesure même où il croira l'avoir desservi. Sa naïveté aura raison de tout, et il mourra tranquillement d'un cancer.[2]

In the same month he sent the opening fifty pages of the novel to Valéry-Radot together with a covering letter which outlined in slightly greater detail not only the substance of the book but also its intended impact:

> Vous devinez que mon ami [le curé] va être cerné par un village en révolte. Mais cette révolte sera sourde, et lui n'en prendra jamais conscience. Et puis, il y a ce bienheureux cancer.
> Je voudrais aussi que ce petit village fût un 'condensé' de notre pays—le châtelain, l'adjoint, l'épicier, les gosses je les vois tous. Et parmi eux,

[1] For the fullest treatment of this to date see Michel Estève, 'Genèse du *Journal d'un curé de campagne*', *Etudes bernanosiennes*, No. 2, pp. 5–15.

[2] *Bernanos par lui-même*, pp. 173,4.

quelques âmes très chères qui s'ignorent [elles-mêmes] et s'ignorent entre elles, ne se rencontrent qu'en Dieu, sans le savoir.[3]

Pressed by his publisher and also by his own financial dilemma Bernanos was obliged to leave the *Journal d'un curé de campagne* at this point in order to finish *Un Crime* and *Un Mauvais Rêve*, and although impatient to do so[4] it was not until September 1935 that he gave it his undivided attention and completed it in January of the following year.

Eventually published in March 1936 by Plon, the whole of the *Journal d'un curé de campagne* was first serialized by the *Revue hebdomadaire* from November 1935 until February 1936.[5] For those whose ambition it is to discover actual events and personalities behind an author's fictional world, the châtelain of Bernanos' native Fressin, whose daughter perceived some of his characteristics in the comte, provides a good example. Bernanos readily admitted to this but he also pointed out that her father 'n'est pas absent non plus du personnage (qui m'est si cher) du curé de Torcy'.[6] More significant still, however, and as his critics have often indicated, is that Bernanos, like his fellow Catholic novelist Mauriac, constantly draws on his childhood memories for inspiration.[7] It is these memories, particularly of the mud and dank climate of his northern regions, which are also to be found in the hitherto unfinished *Monsieur Ouine* and which provide one of the several points of similarity between this novel and the *Journal d'un curé de campagne*.

While not linked in the manner of Gide's 'twin novels' *L'Immoraliste* and *La Porte étroite*, these two works are not Bernanos' first attempt to write a pair of novels related to one another in a fairly detailed manner.

---

[3] *Bernanos par lui-même*, p. 174.    [4] *Bernanos par lui-même*, p. 175.

[5] Both Michel Estève and Dr. O'Sharkey seem to be of the opinion that only the first chapters of the novel were serialized. See *Etudes bernanosiennes*, No. 2, p. 9; *Œuvres romanesques*, p. 1846 ('Les premiers chapitres de ce roman apparaissent dans la *Revue hebdomadaire*.') and O'Sharkey, Edition, p. 21. As it stands the *Revue hebdomadaire* text omits a number of important episodes which are contained both in the original manuscript and in the final book version. I have been unable to discover on whose authority these cuts were made.

[6] *Etudes bernanosiennes*, No. 2, p. 10.

[7] *Etudes bernanosiennes*, p. 10: 'Des que je prends la plume ce qui se lève tout de suite en moi, c'est mon enfance, mon enfance si ordinaire, qui ressemble à toutes les autres, et dont pourtant je tire tout ce que j'écris comme une source inépuisable de rêves.'

Already in 1927 and 1929 *L'Imposture* and *La Joie* emerged as complementary works; the apostasy of Cénabre being redeemed partly by the suffering of Chevance in the former, but more particularly by that of Chantal de Clergerie in the latter.[8] There is considerable justification for viewing *Monsieur Ouine* and the *Journal d'un curé de campagne* in the same way; indeed one critic, Hans Aaraas, expresses this rather neatly when he compares them to the two panels of a diptych:

> Ces deux œuvres maîtresses de Bernanos forment en effet une espèce de diptyque dont les deux panneaux font s'affronter la paroisse illusoire du professeur de langues et la vraie paroisse du prêtre d'Ambricourt.[9]

Aaraas' words have doubtless been prompted by Albert Béguin's earlier view of Ouine himself:

> La véritable figure sacerdotale, ici, ne l'est que par antiphrase, puisque c'est celle de M. Ouine lui-même, qui occupe exactement la place du prêtre, mais dans une paroisse qui, comme l'indiquait le premier titre du livre, est une *paroisse morte*.[10]

Unfortunately Béguin was unable to take this interpretation further, but it is enough to suggest that there is a much closer relationship between these two books than has so far been recognized. The abbé Pezeril added substance to the theory when he indicated the similarity of biographical detail in the portraits of the two priests, the curé de Fenouille and the curé d'Ambricourt; more importantly he has also shown that the *Journal d'un curé de campagne* opens on the themes of *ennui* and solitude, the same as were under discussion at the point where Bernanos abandoned *Monsieur Ouine*.[11]

Relevant as Pezeril's observations are, however, a careful reading of the two novels suggests that the relationship between them is even more extensive. *Monsieur Ouine* is the story of a village in which the apparently gratuitous murder of a young swine-herd provokes suspicion and tension

---

[8] Bernanos had at one time hoped that the two novels would form a single volume. Cf. *Bernanos par lui-même*, p. 162: 'quel roman eût été *L'Imposture* et *La Joie* si le temps m'avait été laissé de fondre les deux volumes en un seul'.

[9] Aaraas, p. 21.    [10] *Bernanos par lui-même*, p. 78.

[11] *Bulletin de la société des Amis de Georges Bernanos*, Nos. 35–6, Paris, April, 1960. Cf. *Etudes bernanosiennes*, No. 2, p. 10.

B

in such a way that the evil that is latent in the community gradually comes to the surface causing further accusation, suicide and even murder. Monsieur Ouine himself is an ambiguous figure who resides in the local chateau. It is suggested that he is guilty of the crime, but whatever the answer may be, and the mystery is never solved, it is the emergent evil for which he appears to be responsible that is important. Surrounded by corruption the priest is powerless; he is relegated to a position of total ineffectiveness and the evil which lurks permanently beneath the surface breaks out around him even in his church:

> L'église a perdu sa douce odeur de résine, de mousse et de feuillage flétri. Elle est sombre et chaude comme une étable. De l'abside la lumière des cierges vient traîner sur les dalles de la nef, rampe le long des piliers de pierre toujours suants d'une eau glacée, d'une eau morte qui graisse les mains, puis elle achève de se perdre sous les voûtes.[12]

While there is not the space here to undertake the type of comparative study that these two books deserve, it is useful and indeed important that the extent of their similarity be grasped if Bernanos' intentions in the *Journal d'un curé de campagne* are to be properly understood. We are at once aware in *Monsieur Ouine* of the use Bernanos makes of the weather to mirror a spiritual state, of the interminable dialogue and struggle between good and evil, of the neatly disguised cross-section of society, and in particular his denunciation of all mediocrity and rejection of God. There are as well a number of fairly detailed similarities in addition to those noted by Pezeril: for example both Ouine and the curé d'Ambricourt (though with different emotions) view their respective villages from a vantage point and the two priests are met with the same peasant indifference to religion.

More than in any other novel by Bernanos, however, we find in *Monsieur Ouine* an almost total capitulation in favour of evil. Purity and innocence are all but lost for ever: 'Le monde ne sera bientôt que pourriture et gangrène. Pourriture et gangrène', remarks the priest.[13] Ouine's photograph of himself as a boy has become significantly worn over the years: 'L'image est si fripée, si jaunie, qu'on y distingue à peine un collégien court de manches, court de culotte et déjà trop gras.'[14] Jambe de Laine's hand may still be described as 'pure', but it is 'sous la boue

---

[12] *Monsieur Ouine*, Livre de Poche edition, 1963, p. 166.
[13] *Monsieur Ouine*, p. 177.      [14] *Monsieur Ouine*, p. 93.

et le cambouis';[15] similarly, while the childlike simplicity of her features may be glimpsed, it is only for a moment:

> Elle incline la tête, découvre à travers la chevelure remplie d'ombre un profil d'une incroyable pureté. Chaque trait de son visage s'est détendu, repose, et la bouche enfantine a l'air de s'ouvrir à une eau mystérieuse.[16]

Both Ouine himself and Arsène, the mayor of Fenouille, are obsessed with corruption, their own and that of the world as a whole, but Ouine's manic cleaning of his room, his own scrupulously clean appearance and his nervous tic of brushing himself are only a thin façade concealing the dirt and corruption that lie beneath:

> La chambre de M. Ouine est tapissée de papier rose un peu fané, mais propre, et il a lui-même blanchi le plafond à la chaux. Malheureusement la crasse séculaire reparaît sous les badigeons, y dessine des caps, des golfes, des îles, toute une géographie mystérieuse.[17]

Arsène hopes in vain to find spiritual relief through physical cleanliness:

> L'odeur que je veux dire n'est pas véritablement une odeur, ça vient de plus loin, de plus profond, de la mémoire, de l'âme, est-ce qu'on sait? L'eau n'y fait rien, faudrait autre chose.[18]

We also have the impression that evil is all embracing, through the references to the ever-present sickly sweet atmosphere, whether in Ouine's room or in the presbytery. The ambivalent sexual relationships of Sweeny's home are also extended throughout the book, and Ouine himself, decaying internally, finally dies but only after having ensured that Sweeny will continue as his disciple.

Most noticeable of all, however, is the way in which, as Béguin observes, Ouine is dominant in his role of anti-priest. The curé is only a shadow of his heroic forebears—Donissan, Chevance and Chantal de Clergerie—and, as we might expect, his role is reduced to an absolute minimum. He does not appear until over half-way in the book, by which time the forces of evil have been well and truly set in motion. Moreover,

---

[15] *Monsieur Ouine*, p. 69.       [16] *Monseiur Ouine*, p. 96.
[17] *Monseiur Ouine*, p. 21.
[18] *Monsieur Ouine*, p. 115. The curé de Torcy makes the same point; *Journal d'un curé de campagne*, p. 14.

he is allowed to occupy less than one-third of the novel and only occasionally to be successful in communicating with his village. On the first of his major appearances he is completely dominated by Ouine who insists that the essentially corrupt state of mankind is proved by the catalytic effect of the murder. He encourages the curé to admit to the helplessness of his position and to his isolation, and in doing so induces the self-pity that must at all costs be avoided. The episode featuring the sermon and grave scene is the only one where he has any success in arousing a sense of self awareness in his congregation, but it is short-lived and, ironically, he only serves to incite his parishioners to murder. Evil has swamped him completely and he can only look on helplessly: 'On remarqua que le prêtre toujours silencieux ne releva même pas la tête. Quelques-uns crurent qu'il pleurait.'[19] Such failure here, however unintentional and ironic, is prolonged later in the book in his dealings with the doctor and Arsène. In his conversation with the former his anxious references to the apocalyptic beasts who will come to root out evil, and even his insistence on the value of faith, only achieve a momentary degree of effectiveness and he emerges from this scene as though from a dream.[20] His influence on Arsène is equally insubstantial. To the mayor's anguished plea for guidance on absolution and salvation he has no adequate reply, and his last despairing words, 'Qu'ai-je fait?',[21] when he and the doctor discover that Arsène has escaped from the presbytery presumably in order to kill himself, are to be expected from a man who has so clearly failed in his vocation.[22] At this point in the novel the curé disappears and Ouine is left to dominate the remaining pages in a way that the former had proved quite incapable of doing.

As Professor Bush has observed, it is likely that Bernanos abandoned *Monsieur Ouine* during the conversation between the curé and Arsène because he felt that at this point he was too deeply committed to a portrayal of evil and could see no easy escape.[23] But this does not explain why, when he took up the novel again, the earlier themes should

[19] *Monseuir Ouine*, p. 181.

[20] *Monseiur Ouine*, p. 198. Cf. his feelings after the sermon, p. 167.

[21] *Monseiur Ouine*, p. 218. Compare with the scene between Chantal and the cure in the *Journal d'un curé de campagne*, p. 173.

[22] That Arsène has found his way to God unaided is indicated by his final message written in the dust (ADIEU), and also by its being described as 'un dessin *puéril*' (p. 218). My italics.

[23] Bush, *Angoisse du mystère*, p. 25.

re-emerge with as much force as before. It is as though the curé's words
had indeed been prophetic:

> L'heure vient où sur les ruines de ce qui reste encore de l'ancien ordre
> chrétien, le nouvel ordre va naître qui sera réellement l'ordre du
> Monde, l'ordre du Prince du Monde, du prince dont le royaume est
> en ce Monde.[24]

The action of the three final chapters occurs entirely in Ouine's room
where the presence of the midwife symbolically underlines the emergence
of Steeny as Ouine's disciple. Evil is guaranteed to continue and the
curé's earlier words have again proved significant: 'C'est long à tuer, une
paroisse! Celle-ci aura tenu jusqu'au bout. Maintenant elle est morte.'[25]

It is against this depiction of total evil that the emphasis of the *Journal
d'un curé de campagne* becomes important. The curé d'Ambricourt
succeeds where the curé de Fenouille fails, precisely through his willingness to struggle; unlike his fellow priest he resists the temptation to
succumb to self-pity[26] and fights the evil which surrounds him both in
Ambricourt and in Lille. Yves Bridel, discussing Bernanos' changed
attitude, writes, 'Nous voyons Fenouille à travers l'angoisse et peut-être
le désespoir de l'auteur; nois voyons Ambricourt à travers la charité,
l'espérance et la foi du curé et de Bernanos.'[27] But in order to inject these
themes of faith, hope and charity into his new novel with any success
Bernanos has to alter his technique of novel writing, and it is in the
manipulation of his material that he succeeds in creating the work that
provides the perfect antidote to the pessimistic message of *Monsieur
Ouine*.

[24] *Monsieur Ouine*, pp. 179,80.      [25] *Monseiur Ouine*, p. 170.
[26] *Monsieur Ouine*, p. 203.      [27] Bridel, p. 143.

# 3. Technique

Of all the distinctive stylistic features of Bernanos' writing, literary and journalistic alike, the one that is most immediately noticeable is its episodic and even, at times, fragmentary nature. While this may legitimately be considered more appropriate in journalism, we find it just as evident in his novels where it allows the action to move from one crucial issue to another with little or none of the linking commentary of the sort we normally expect. From the *Histoire de Mouchette*, the elaborate opening part of *Sous le soleil de Satan*,[1] to *Monsieur Ouine*, in which chapters often appear to have a minimum of logical sequence, it is relatively easy to extract any number of examples varying in length from a few pages to an entire section of a novel—Donissan's attempt to bring Madame Havret's son back to life in *Sous le soleil de Satan*; Cénabre's meeting and conversation with the tramp in *L'Imposture*; Olivier's appearance in the *Journal d'un curé de campagne* and many more besides. Such a method has certain advantages. The reader is never allowed to become hypnotized by a monotone account; instead his attention is continually and often sharply drawn to the particular points which the author is trying to convey. In view of this it is all the more surprising therefore that Bernanos should turn for the first time, as late in his career as the mid-thirties, to two techniques which enable him to project personal convictions through a medium that is by its very nature both intimate and episodic—the private diary or *journal intime*.

As a literary form in its own right the *journal intime* has a long and substantial tradition. In the eighteenth and nineteenth centuries Maine de Biran, Constant and Stendhal were, among others, its major exponents, while in more recent years Gide and Jouhandeau have ensured its continuation. In approaching Bernanos and the *Journal d'un curé de campagne*, however, our concern should be for the problems and advantages of the diary disguised as a novel, and more generally with the use and value of the first person as a narrative method. In adopting this Bernanos is again following a strong tradition which looks back to such eminent precursors as *La Vie de Marianne*, *Adolphe*, or *Dominique*, and which also appears

[1] See A. Sonnenfeld, 'The Art of Georges Bernanos: The Prologue to *Sous le soleil de Satan*', *Orbis Literarum*, 1967, xxi, pp. 133–53.

regularly in the work of a number of leading contemporary novelists. In spite of such widespread use, and even though novelists often resort to this method in order to by-pass laborious explanations and justifications for their characters' actions or decisions, its function is neither as limited nor as stereotyped as it might at first appear. Such recent novels as Sartre's *La Nausée*, Mauriac's *Le Nœud de vipères*, Gide's *L'Immoraliste* or *La Symphonie pastorale* and Camus' *La Chute*, for example, are all quite different not only in what they set out to achieve but also in their application of the first person narrative. The first three may be considered in one respect as works which, through the hero's personal account and interpretation of certain experiences, seek to convince us of their validity; the final two on the other hand contain a much clearer built-in critical apparatus which turns, often by implication, upon the positions and views held by the narrator. The hypocrisy of the Pasteur and Clamence's role as a confidence trickster are never in doubt, even though these facts are not set out for us explicitly. In spite of the introduction of such autocriticism (or irony as Gide would call it), novelists are also clearly quite aware that the first person technique has its dangers. By delaying the disclosure of Rieux's identification in *La Peste* until the end of the book, for example, Camus is admitting that a first person account of life in Oran could have appeared biased. In *Les Anges noirs* Mauriac turns from Gradère's diary to actual events in order, so it seems, to avoid charges of falsification and partiality over a matter as delicate as conversion, especially when the diary has been written for Alain Forcas, the young priest, as a confession and plea by Gradère for his essential innocence.

Bernanos' predicament is similar. In view of the enthusiastic and vigorous way in which he characteristically translates his personal convictions into the language of his novels, it is possible that he considered the first person narrative technique at some point in his career only to discard it as unsuitable since it would open to him the criticism of facile didacticism that as a novelist he wished to avoid. On the other hand, however, his critics, particularly the Catholic ones, expected his books to be in some way monuments to his faith, but Bernanos was enough of a novelist to realize that certain subjects were beyond the scope of the novel. Together with his fellow Catholic novelists, Mauriac and Julien Green, he believed that if they were to write meaningfully for their readers they could only draw on a limited range of shared experiences or emotions. However much he or anyone else may be assured of God's love or the power of divine Grace, these, grasped only through faith, remain essentially personal matters and hence outside the easy definition of the printed word. Less readily disturbed than Mauriac by the criticism that in portraying evil and sin he was betraying the Catholic faith, and not as prepared, it seems, to hide behind Green's excuse that his two existences as Catholic and novelist were essentially quite separate, Bernanos sought to provoke his readers into a re-examination of established attitudes towards religion. One way was to bring home to them the very real presence and nature of evil in the world, for in contrast to this the exemplary faith of his saints is seen to be much more positive than the anaemic complacency of much of the established church. And yet, with *Monsieur Ouine* and the failure in this novel of the curé de Fenouille to do more than protest against the forces of evil, Bernanos reached an impasse. *La Joie* had already proved to him that a passive display of purity and innocence was not sufficiently convincing; what was needed instead was a positive though not didactic statement of the efficacy of faith and love, and the use of a priest's private diary provided him with the ideal form of expression.

Unlike Louis' in *Le Nœud de vipères* or Gradère's in *Les Anges noirs*, the curé's diary is not consciously intended for other people. Bernanos aims to create the impression of a spontaneously written private diary discovered, unbeknown to the author, after his death. In this way the curé's reflections and theories, his interpretation of his own and other people's actions, and his relationship with God are presented in a totally authentic manner. Should he choose to do so, Bernanos is in a position to identify himself wholly with his priest without risking the accusation of shaping his narrative to suit his (Bernanos') particular end. It is possible and quite legitimate, of course, for us to object to Bernanos' personal interpretation of faith or even to the more easily definable question of his view of the priest's role in the world, but such an objection can only be made *in abstracto* outside the limits of the book. By employing the private diary in this way Bernanos turns our attention from the ideas to their means of expression. Like Gide, for whom, ironically, he had little more than contempt, Bernanos is in a position to argue that the only grounds on which his book can be judged are literary ones. He had already had sufficient experience in novel writing, however, to realize that diaries do not necessarily make successful novels, and a careful examination of the *Journal d'un curé de campagne* reveals that it is much more carefully constructed than it at first appears.

In the main its critics have contented themselves with general statements with little adequate illustration to support them. Dr. O'Sharkey for example writes: 'The diary form itself helps to give unity to the novel. . . . The *Journal* has, indeed, all the spontaneity and disorder of a real diary.'[2] She also maintains, rightly enough, that the various characters who appear are never fully revealed to us, though she fails to point out that this must be accepted as part of Bernanos' aim to present his readers with the single unifying interpretation that a *journal intime* necessarily involves. Peter Hebblethwaite, who sees the benefits to be gained in this form of narration, refers to the 'apparently random outpourings of a wholly dedicated man, who speaks directly to God. . . . There is no omniscient narrator to intrude with his nudges and explanations.'[3] Yves Bridel on the other hand argues that

> nous avons affaire à un roman, avec des personnages ayant leur vie propre, et avec une action habilement agencée. . . . Le *Journal d'un curé de campagne* est un roman composé avec soin et où la présence de l'auteur est constante.[4]

In spite of their incompleteness, such statements as these acknowledge, if only implicitly, the way in which Bernanos has succeeded in allowing us to glimpse the deeper, skilfully balanced arrangement of his material adumbrated in the diary form. As we can see from the remarks above, his attempts to create the impression of freedom and spontaneity have met with success. There is no fixed time pattern for example:[5] the curé d'Ambricourt sets a limit of twelve months (p. 8), which is not kept, for he dies the following February. No more is there any standardization in the size of the entries, which appear to vary from a few lines to well over twenty pages. Bernanos also has an eye for more subtle matters of detail. Pages torn out by the curé in moments of anger or despair are not uncommon and after one such break we find the text taken up again in the middle of one of his recorded conversations with the curé de Torcy.[6] Allusions are made to events which have not been recorded elsewhere; the argument he has had with Dumouchel the sacristain over the prices of

[2] O'Sharkey, Edition, p. 51.     [3] Hebblethwaite, p. 74.
[4] Bridel, p. 145 and p. 147.
[5] In the *Revue hebdomadaire* version the diary entries contained between p. 43 and p. 58 in the Plon edition are dated from 17 November until 11 December. There is no such dating in the manuscript.
[6] p. 244.

candles and other church furnishings, the reference to the badger which the comte has killed in his presence, or to his 'deuxième syncope'.[7] And above all we are made aware of the exclusiveness of the curé's field of vision by the deliberate and carefully noted selection of other people's opinions and interpretations. Delbende for example emerges principally through Torcy's description of him (p. 145), and Torcy himself is given an extra dimension by the café owner's opinion of him, even if it does bear out what we know of him already.[8] More significant still, however, is Chantal's account of the interview which the curé has with her mother and which we are not actually given but can glean from the recorded statements of others,[9] for in this way Bernanos is able to remind us of the extra dimensions of his subject that are hidden behind the superficial diary form.[10]

Beyond such features as these and opening the way for a deeper investigation of the *Journal d'un curé de campagne* lies the curé's personal concern for the reliability and the purpose of his diary. He constantly appeals through himself to an imaginary reader:

A lire ces lignes, on pensera sans doute que je ne parlais pas au hasard, que je suivais un plan. Il n'était rien, je le jure. (p. 204)[11]

He also shows himself to be awake to the dangers of writing, of creating an illusionary dream world in which to take shelter and thereby avoid his own spiritual dilemma:[12]

Pour quiconque a l'habitude de la prière, la réflexion n'est trop souvent qu'un alibi. (p. 6)

la principale, ou peut-être la seule utilité de ce journal sera de m'entretenir dans les habitudes d'entière franchise envers moi-même. (p. 43)

---

[7] pp. 10, 169, 343.        [8] pp. 319,20.

[9] Torcy, who himself is reporting what he has heard, remarks: 'Forcer une mère à jeter au feu le seul souvenir qu'elle garde d'un enfant mort, cela ressemble à une histoire juive, c'est de l'Ancien Testament' (p. 250).

[10] We must also accept less subtly disguised features: the curé's ability to reproduce certain conversations at length, detailed arguments and complex theories; full summaries or reproductions of Dufréty's letters where a reference might have been enough; and even an account of his own delirium (pp. 260 ff).

[11] Cf. pp. 173, 197, 201.        [12] Aaraas, p. 8.

His diary becomes increasingly an instrument of self-analysis, revealing to him his sense of helplessness and weakness:

> Qui ne comprendrait d'ailleurs, ne serait-ce qu'à la lecture de ces pages misérables où ma faiblesse, ma honteuse faiblesse, éclate à chaque ligne. (p. 175)[13]

But, however painful, the process is all important for the curé, who is forced instead to seek strength through his faith, and the diary becomes a direct link between himself and God, 'une conversation entre le bon Dieu et moi, un prolongement de la prière' (p. 29). Above all, however, this element of self awareness in turn allows us an important advantage, for, while given the limits of the diary we may accept the curé's account of his actions, we are not obliged to agree with his interpretation of them. In this way a necessary contrast between his view of himself and ours is established. As Hebblethwaite remarks: 'The reader knows, from the evidence before him that the Curé has succeeded. The Curé thinks that he has failed, and any other judgement on his part would be intolerable, lacking in humanity and humility.'[14]

[13] Cf. pp. 232, 234, 307.
[14] Hebblethwaite, p. 76. And see above, p. 15: 'il aura servi le bon Dieu dans la mesure même où il croira l'avoir desservi'.

# 4. Structure

Beneath these various attempts to create the impression of spontaneity we find, on careful examination, that the *Journal d'un curé de compagne* is constructed in such a way that a number of elements become evident, all interlocking and dependent on one another if they are to be fully appreciated. In many cases they are not clearly distinguishable, a tribute to the complexity of Bernanos' writing, but they can nonetheless be outlined sufficiently for us also to appreciate the constant control that he has over his material.

## (a) *Form*

In dividing the *Journal d'un curé de campagne* into its three parts Bernanos is following a pattern which, with the exception of *Monsieur Ouine*, exists in all his other novels. In some ways, just as pairs of novels complement one another, so the various parts within individual books appear as tableaux which, when put together, inter-reflect to give us a complex multi-angled treatment of his subject.[1] While in the *Journal d'un curé de campagne* this technique is reduced, since our angle of vision remains for the most part constant, each part still has its own particular function.

The opening section of thirty pages acts as a kind of prologue, and as we might expect, therefore, we are introduced to certain features that will persist throughout the book. In the opening lines, for example, the intended universality of the parish and of the curé's role as its representative at once become apparent:

> Ma paroisse est une paroisse comme les autres. Toutes les paroisses se ressemblent. Les paroisses d'aujourd'hui, naturellement. (p. 1)

Like his fellow priest in *Monsieur Ouine* the curé has no name, his anonymity stripping him of all superficial individual status, and this notion of isolation and responsibility is soon enlarged by Bernanos as the

[1] Milner, p. 95, writes that the three parts of *Sous le soleil de Satan*, for example, offer us 'trois approches de la vérité: une approche psychologique, une approche fantastique, et une approche théologale'.

curé's thoughts on the spiritual aridity of his charge are extended into a statement about mankind as a whole:

> Ma paroisse est dévorée par l'ennui, voilà le mot. Comme tant d'autres paroisses. L'ennui les dévore sous nos yeux et nous n'y pouvons rien. (p. 1)

> Je me disais donc que le monde est dévoré par l'ennui. . . . On dira peut-être que le monde est depuis longtemps familiarisé avec l'ennui, que l'ennui est la véritable condition de l'homme. (p. 3)

In a like manner the subsequent tone of the whole novel is established by translating his awareness of such *ennui* into images of disease and references to the rain and mud around him:

> L'idée m'est venue hier sur la route. Il tombait une de ces pluies fines qu'on avale à pleins poumons, qui vous descendent jusqu'au ventre. De la côte de Saint-Vaast, le village m'est apparu brusquement, si tassé, si misérable sous le ciel hideux de novembre. L'eau fumait sur lui de toutes parts, et il avait l'air de s'être couché là, dans l'herbe ruisselante, comme une pauvre bête épuisée. (p. 2)

Having extended the problem of society and religion in this way from the local and particular to the universal, Bernanos introduces the principal attitudes of the church towards it, and at once the curé de Torcy emerges as the forceful personality he is to remain during the rest of the book. By allowing him to occupy well over half of the opening section Bernanos is able not only to give us a foretaste of his principal theories, but also by implication to underline the all important frailty of the curé d'Ambricourt at this stage.

These opening pages introducing us to the scene of the curé's struggle are balanced by the third section, nearly fifty pages in length, in which he moves out of his parish to Lille; a development seen by some critics to indicate the fact that he is extending his struggle against encroaching evil to the industrial towns, traditionally the centres of dechristianization.[2] More relevant for our present consideration, however, is the way in which these pages fulfil the function of an epilogue. In particular they contain the episode of Dufréty's mistress, which links them significantly to earlier passages dealing with humility and poverty, and which refer to

[2] See in particular Henri Giordan, 'La réalité sociale et politique dans le *Journal d'un curé de campagne*', *Etudes bernanosiennes*, No. 2, pp. 87–121, and Estève, Edition, p. 272.

the Virgin Mary or Joan of Arc. D'Ambricourt's stature is also implied here through the appearance of Dufréty himself, who is an inversion of all that the curé represents. He is a *représentant* (p. 338), a person who betrays himself by pretending to be what he is not; he sells drugs already defined earlier in the book by Torcy as the latest weapons of the Devil,[3] and claims to be able to 'manier les hommes' (p. 346). Perhaps most damning of all, however, is his *cold* hand and his pretentious claim to intellectual superiority evident in his earlier letters and set out for posterity in his autobiographical *Mes Etapes*, which is the exact opposite of the curé's own humble diary.

Held between these two sections is the bulk of the novel, structured around the comtesse episode.[4] In addition to the careful build-up to this scene there are as well a number of major topics and events emerging rather like chapters—Torcy's various visits, the appearance of Delbende, the curé's conversations with Chantal, the episode when he is discovered by Séraphita, the meeting with Olivier, and so on. As we have already seen, one of the advantages of the diary form is precisely that Bernanos can move from one topic to another without concerning himself over-much with any linking commentary. Nevertheless he does appear to be aware that there is a very real danger of alienating his reader with a concentration of intellectually demanding passages with a minimum of relief. Consequently we find that references to the curé's domestic problems, for example, are more frequent before the comtesse scene and that while it is true that such details create a valid human portrait of him, they also lessen the tension. In contrast, after the comtesse scene incidental matters are pruned to a minimum, while the diary entries themselves are on average longer and more intense. Particularly impressive, however, is the manner in which Bernanos develops the climactic pattern of this central portion of the book. From the beginning the chateau looms large and is associated with or contrasted to the presbytery. Until just before this crucial scene it stands as an adversary to be challenged and overcome: 'Le château est sur l'autre versant, il tourne le dos au village, à nous tous' (p. 177). Moreover the actual confrontation with the comtesse not only marks the climax of the curé's mission, but draws together all the central themes of the book and establishes the curé in the Christlike role that is the ultimate aim for all Bernanos' saints. Through its unity—stylistic and structural as well as thematic[5]—this scene is typical of many in the

3 *Journal d'un curé de campagne*, p. 24.    4 Balthasar, p. 353.
5 See below, pp. 47–53.

novel. One other that we should perhaps draw attention to at this point for similar reasons is the curé's meeting with Olivier. Here the sheer physical exaltation that the curé experiences is in marked contrast to his normal life; the strong recollection of childhood coming here shortly before his death is a favourite Bernanos theme, as is the general emphasis on purity, while the style subtly provides an extra dimension through a number of associated words: *clair, or, blanches, éblouissante, soleil*. Moreover the episode is also thematically linked with the appearances of Delbende and, to some extent, of Torcy elsewhere.

At the close of the book we have Dufréty's letter. In Mauriac's *Le Nœud de vipères* the final letters from Hubert to Geneviève and from Janine to Hubert offer two different interpretations of Louis' character and actions, and underline Mauriac's own position in relation to him. In the *Journal d'un curé de campagne* Bernanos uses Dufréty's letter for the same purpose. In addition to providing an objective third person account of an event otherwise unrecordable, it is in its lies, pretentious claims and inflated quasi-medical language in direct contrast to all that is represented by the curé's diary. At the same time, however, it also conveys the interpretation that Bernanos wishes to give to the curé's death. As a demonstration of simplicity and total faith ('"Qu'est-ce que cela fait? Tout est grâce"' (p. 366)), it is a natural and fitting extension to his role throughout the book, and while it appears to have no influence on Dufréty, who remains uncomprehending to the end, for his mistress its effect has been quite different and she has left him, it seems: 'La personne qui partageait *alors* ma vie . . .' (p. 365). More important still, however, is the fact that now after a life fraught with anguish and a sense of inadequacy the curé has at last found peace. His faith has been rewarded and Bernanos' message made clear.

In addition to this formal division of the book there are a number of passages where Bernanos has linked individual scenes together in order to give a rounded view of a particular matter. The size of this study unfortunately precludes an examination of all the examples of this type, but one which will serve as a means of comparison for others is in that section of the novel (pp. 58–91) in which Torcy, the doyen de Blangermont and finally the curé himself consider the role and duty of the church in modern society.

Torcy is here making the second of his appearances in the book and at once the principal lines of his philosophy are set out for us. He stresses that the kingdom of God is not of this world and that, unless modern society is willing to seek it, death and oblivion are the only alternative. He refers nostalgically to the *Ancien Monde* (Jacques Maritain called it a sacral civilization) as a time when the Church and secular society were dependent on one another, and it is with this in mind that he appears to approve of slavery:

> A bien prendre la chose, un esclave coûtait cher, ça devait toujours lui valoir de son maître une certaine considération. (p. 160)

This in turn leads him first to consider the poor, the meek and the humble, who have been glorified by Christ's sharing of their position, and then the notion of childhood with its similar considerations of dependence and trust. Here we find ourselves at the central issue both of this book and of Bernanos' thought as a whole—absolute faith and humility. In sharp contrast is what Torcy defines as the 'esprit de richesse', in the sense not only of material possession but also of the desire to manipulate rather than to protect: 'Il y aura toujours des pauvres parmi vous, pour cette raison qu'il y aura toujours des riches, c'est-à-dire des hommes avides et durs qui recherchent moins la possession que la puissance' (p. 79).

Torcy's appearance, which goes a long way to defining his character, is followed by that of his ecclesiastical superior, the doyen de Blangermont. The contrast is striking and immediate. Blangermont talks at length with the curé of trivial domestic matters, but in particular he is shown to us to be conservative and hostile to any kind of change: 'Dieu nous préserve des réformateurs,'[6] he remarks. Bernanos also heavily underlines Blangermont's view that the church must meet society on the latter's terms, and that it is the material interest of the church that should be primarily considered: 'L'Eglise possède un corps et une âme: il lui faut pourvoir aux besoins de son corps' (p. 85). Nothing could be further removed from Torcy's visionary, if impracticable, plans nor indeed from Bernanos' own. Already in *La Grande Peur des bien-pensants* he had bitterly attacked the attitude of mind which proposed that the Church should compromise with the Republic, on the grounds that this was a betrayal of its essential values, and was to do so again with even more vehemence in the *Grands cimetières sous la lune*.

This section of the book closes with a brief but significant reflection by

---

[6] *Journal d'un curé de campagne*, p. 83. Torcy of course admires Luther; his first name is also Martin.

the curé on the two arguments that have been presented to him. His decision is immediate and clear. He accepts Torcy's views not only because he feels that he needs the elder priest's spiritual support, but also because he is, unbeknown to himself, stigmatized by true poverty. Moreover he translates his decision into the image of the medieval feudal bond that Torcy himself is so fond of using:

> On peut mettre ses deux mains jointes entre les mains d'un autre homme et lui jurer la fidélité du vassal mais l'idée ne viendrait à personne de procéder à cette cérémonie aux pieds d'un millionnaire, parce que millionnaire, ce serait idiot. La notion de richesse et celle de puissance ne peuvent encore se confondre, la première reste abstraite. Je sais bien qu'on aurait beau jeu de répondre que plus d'un seigneur a dû jadis son fief aux sacs d'écus d'un père usurier, mais enfin, acquis ou non à la pointe de l'épée, c'est à la pointe de l'épée qu'il devait le défendre comme il eût défendu sa propre vie, car l'homme et le fief ne faisaient qu'un, au point de porter le même nom . . . (p. 90)

In these pages, as indeed elsewhere in the book, it is the novelist, aware of the impact he wishes to make through his work and in consequence consciously shaping it, whom we can glimpse behind the superficially random style and structure of the diary. It is in a sense ironic, therefore, that the one book in which his aim was to create an impression of spontaneity should be much more purposefully constructed than any of his others.

## (b) *Characters*

Unlike *Sous le soleil de Satan*, in which the influence of Bernanos' early reading of Balzac can still occasionally be seen, the *Journal d'un curé de campagne* offers us very little detailed physical description of the various characters with whom the curé comes into contact. As Etienne-Alain Hubert observes:

> les personnages n'y font jamais l'objet d'une description suivie . . . le romancier ne décrit jamais ses héros, mais les fait apparaître dans leurs traits significatifs selon que l'exige la nécessité interne du récit.[7]

[7] 'L'expression romanesque du surnaturel dans le *Journal d'un curé de campagne*', *Etudes bernanosiennes*, No. 2, p. 29 and p. 40. Cf. O'Sharkey, Edition, p. 40.

C

At once the usefulness of the diary form becomes re-apparent, for it is quite within the bounds of authenticity that the curé should mention only those features of other people which strike him (and therefore us). Moreover he is consistent in his observations, so that characters who appear on a number of different occasions—Torcy or the comtesse, for example—do so in a familiar way, while others who are only episodic— Olivier, Delbende or Dufréty's mistress—are linked with one another not only by what they represent but also through the curé's descriptions of them. In this way Bernanos ensures that, while each character is enough of an individual to hold our attention as a person and not simply as the embodiment of a particular idea, we are not side-tracked by unnecessary detail. He is able to turn what would have been a private theoretical discussion into a tense human affair and so realize his intention that the village of Ambricourt should represent 'un condensé de notre pays'. The result is an allegorization of the conflict between good and evil that is less melodramatic than the struggle between Donissan and the Devil disguised as a horse dealer in *Sous le soleil de Satan*. At the same time it is not a new technique for Bernanos. Already in his first novel Mouchette is a victim of a number of quite different social environments—her peasant home, the local aristocracy in the form of Cadignan and the unbelieving world of medicine and republicanism in Gallet. Similarly in *Monsieur Ouine* we find a complete range of social figures from the swine-herd or Guillaume to the decadent châtelain, each in turn having been assigned by Bernanos to a particular role. In the *Journal d'un curé de campagne* the same pattern re-emerges—on the one hand a secular rural and urban society which at best only accepts the outward show of religion[8] and on the other a range of ecclesiastics whose sense of duty and commitment varies more in this than in any of Bernanos' other novels.

Without oversimplifying Bernanos' intentions it is possible to subdivide the secular society of the *Journal d'un curé de campagne* in much the same way as in *Monsieur Ouine*. Four groups at once become evident: those who care only for their material comfort; the militants who while not possessing the curé's faith are sympathetic to his aims and views; those who possess the capacity and the qualities necessary for sainthood, but whose innocence is being slowly corrupted; and finally Dufréty, who is the complete antithesis of the curé. The first of these groups

[8] Michel Estève, 'Une présentation du *Journal d'un curé de campagne* de Georges Bernanos', *Le Français dans le monde*, No. 11, Sept. 1962, p. 47.

extends from the peasant parishioners in Ambricourt to the comte and his family. For Arsène the sacristain, the curé is 'comme un notaire. Il est là en cas de besoin' (p. 240), and to the curé's suggestion that a priest should be exemplary in leading people to God he is totally indifferent. For him official membership of the Church is sufficient: 'Chacun naît tel ou tel, meurt de même. Nous autres dans la famille, nous sommes d'église. . . . Quand on est mort, tout est mort' (p. 241), and this, the older generation's indifference, is paralleled by the young people's resistance to the curé's plans to organize their leisure time (p. 33). At the opposite end of the social scale the comte looks to the Church in much the same way. Typical of the Right wing members of his generation (that of the late nineteenth century) he regards it as one of the mainstays of society; 'la principale mission de l'Eglise est de protéger la famille, la société, elle réprouve tous les excès, elle est une puissance d'ordre, de mesure' (p. 238). He believes in stability and in conservatism, but his urbanity and graceful living, which at first easily dupe the curé (though not Torcy), conceal the 'lust and hatred, pride and resentment'[9] that have eaten the heart out of his family and which even with the comtesse's death do not necessarily come to an end.

In marked contrast to such complacency and spiritual indifference are those who, disgusted by the values of modern society, have opted for a different life, and it is perhaps significant that the three characters who most readily fall into this category—Delbende, Olivier and Laville—do not belong to the curé's parish, for in this way they are not his immediate spiritual concern even though as unbelievers they are sympathetically portrayed. While they are linked together, however, each of the three men retains his individuality. Delbende, like his friend Torcy, is a man of passion. In spite of having lost his faith 'au cours de ses études de médecine' (p. 144) he has retained a deep love-hate relationship with Christianity. He recognizes it as an important social force, but believes (as indeed did Bernanos) that by coming to terms with the rich in order to gain material benefit the Church is guilty of having abandoned the poor.[10] With this in mind we can see that in creating the character of Delbende Bernanos had Drumont in mind, for much of what he expresses through the doctor is an echo of his bitterness in the *Grande Peur des bien-pensants*. Certainly his lack of faith is important; he has, as

[9] O'Sharkey, Edition, pp. 24,5. Cf. Estève, *Le Français dans le monde*, p. 47.
[10] *Journal d'un curé de campagne*, pp. 101–5.

Michel Estève remarks, a conception of the Church that is 'trop maurras-sienne',[11] but he is not a negative character. He is deliberately linked with both Torcy and the curé—'Torcy, vous et moi, nous sommes de la même race, une drôle de race. . . . Celle qui tient debout' (p. 99)[12]—and while the suspicion of suicide does hold against him Torcy is ready to entrust him to God's mercy: 'Maxence . . . était un homme juste. Dieu juge les justes' (p. 145).

Olivier, the comte's nephew, fills a similar role. Equally appalled by the injustice of modern society he too has rebelled by joining the Foreign Legion. In a sense, therefore, his rebellion in practical terms is negative, but it is for his ideals rather than his actions that he wins the curé's sympathy. Together with Torcy[13] he favours the idea of a militant Christianity and looks to the Middle Ages (and to Joan of Arc as its most perfect expression) as a time when it was allowed to flourish. He too, however, firmly believes that such a spirit is now dead and that society has been overcome by the 'esprit de richesse' which, as we have already seen, Bernanos deplores:

> la chrétienté n'appartient plus à personne. Il n'y a plus, il n'y aura plus jamais de chrétienté. (p. 299)

> . . . La cité antique est morte, elle est morte comme ses dieux. Et les dieux proctecteurs de la cité moderne, on les connaît, ils dînent en ville, et s'appellent des banquiers. (p. 303)

His affinity with the young priest is immediately recognizable; they are equals in their sharing of poverty.

The third member of this group of outsiders is Laville, the doctor whom the curé visits by mistake when he goes to Lille. This figure has been almost completely neglected by critics of the book, no doubt because of Bernanos' standard dismissal of doctors and psychologists as people who pretentiously claim to understand human nature. Laville is also a drug addict. Yet between him and the young curé there is an immediate bond of sympathy and understanding: 'Le regard du docteur ne quittait pas le mien, j'y lisais la confiance, la sympathie, je ne sais quoi

---

[11] Estève, *Bernanos*, Paris, 1965, p. 108; *Le Français dans le monde*, p. 47. Cf. *Etudes bernanosiennes*, No. 2, pp. 92 ff. and Milner, p. 198.

[12] Cf. p. 101: 'la station verticale ne (convient) qu'aux Puissants'.

[13] *Journal d'un curé de campagne*, p. 341: 'Je rapproche exprès ces deux noms.'

encore. C'était le regard d'un ami, d'un compagnon' (p. 334). Through-out the episode there are references to their similarity: they are physically alike (p. 321); they come from the same social background (p. 327); Laville senses the fascination that suicide has had for the curé (p. 329); they are both soon to die and as the curé leaves they shake hands (p. 336). Laville is right: 'En vous voyant, tout à l'heure, j'ai eu l'impression désagréable de me trouver devant . . . devant mon double' (p. 327), but he is the curé's *negative* double. Unlike Olivier, whose sense of the world's injustice has caused him to opt out, Laville has succumbed to the easy solution of passive, negative acceptance: 'Il faut apprendre à vivre avec son mal, nous en sommes tous là, plus ou moins' (p. 323). Society has beaten him and he chooses to hasten his death through the use of drugs. He is a victim, but Bernanos' obvious sympathy for him turns our scorn away from his weakness towards the society that has induced it.

The third group of characters who form this side of the pattern are those whose essential innocence and purity is still to be glimpsed behind the corrupting influence of society—Séraphita, Chantal, Dufréty's mistress and to a lesser extent Mlle Louise the *institutrice*. All of these and in particular Chantal are, as Yves Bridel observes, subject to 'le même processus de dégradation de (leur) pureté et de (leur) esprit d'enfance, que celui que nous avons observé chez Germaine Malorthy' in *Sous le soleil de Satan*.[14] In Séraphita the change is noted by the curé:

> Le visage de cette petite me semble se transformer de jour en jour: jadis si changeant, si mobile, je lui trouve maintenant une espèce de fixité, de dureté bien au-dessus de son âge. . . . Je ne pouvais détacher les yeux de son visage. Tout y est flétri, presque vieillot, sauf le front, resté si pur.[15]

Together with Chantal and Mlle Louise she too is an innocent victim of a godless world and she clearly looks forward to Mouchette in the *Nouvelle Histoire de Mouchette*.[16] And yet some hope remains. She is fascinated by the curé's innocence and purity as though these qualities find a distant echo within her own mind, and the way in which she is linked with the Virgin Mary when she discovers him after he has

[14] Bridel, p. 173.
[15] *Journal d'un curé de campagne*, p. 37 and p. 270. Cf. the curé's description of Chantal, p. 92: 'elle a dans ses traits la même fixité, la même dureté que je retrouve, hélas, sur le visage de beaucoup de jeunes gens'.
[16] Bridel, p. 170.

collapsed is just as important for our understanding of the value Bernanos places on childhood as it is for the interpretation of this particular scene. In the third section of the book Dufréty's mistress, gentle, motherlike and humble, also emerges in much the same way though without Séraphita's already well developed streak of viciousness:

> Elle est si petite qu'on la prendrait volontiers pour une de ces fillettes qu'on voit dans les corons et auxquelles il est difficile de donner un âge . . . ses yeux bleus fanés ont un sourire si résigné, si humble, qu'ils ressemblent à des yeux d'aïeule, des yeux de vieille fileuse. (p. 348)[17]

Like the curé himself (and Christ) she shares the burdens of the poor:

> je pense à tous ces gens que je ne connais pas, qui me ressemblent—et il y en a, la terre est grande!—les mendiants qui battent la semelle sous la pluie, les gosses perdus, les malades, les fous des asiles qui gueulent à la lune, et tant! et tant! Je me glisse parmi eux, je tâche de me faire petite, et pas seulement les vivants, vous savez? les morts aussi, qui ont souffert, et ceux à venir, qui souffriront comme nous. . . . Dans ces moments-là, je ne changerais pas une place pour celle d'un millionnaire, je me sens heureuse. (p. 354)

She too is the complete antithesis of Dufréty, with whom she lives, her humility in particular being sharply contrasted with his pretentious claim of having undergone an 'évolution intellectuelle'. Indeed Dufréty's life is based entirely on misrepresentation and deceit.[18] Like the novelists portrayed by Bernanos in other works—St. Marin or Ganse, for example—Dufréty has fabricated an illusionary existence, all the more deplorable in view of his originally intended vocation, and in doing so has become the totally negative reflection of what the curé represents.

Set against these divisions within the secular society of the novel are those of the clergy—the mediocre priests, Torcy the idealist and the curé himself. As we might expect the first of these are characterized, like their secular counterparts, by their complacency and their need for security.

---

[17] Cf. the curé's further description of Chantal, p. 163: 'C'est presque une petite fille, après tout.'

[18] I would disagree with Dr. O'Sharkey who, largely on account of Dufréty's administering of the last sacrament to the curé, includes him in her consideration of the clergy portrayed in the book. See 'Portraits of the Clergy in Bernanos *Diary of a Country Priest*', *Dublin Review*, No. 504, Summer, 1965, pp. 183–91. It is Bernanos' intention to underline the complete divergence of their two lives and careers.

Reflecting on the priests who attend the weekly meeting in Hébuterne to hear a lecture on the Church in the sixteenth century, the curé is shocked by their indifference (p. 39). But just as Arsène and the comte are intended to express the same basic attitude in different ways so differences are to be found between various clerics. The description of the curé de Norenfontes, for example, reminds us of the curé de Fenouille in *Monsieur Ouine:*

> un bon prêtre, très bienveillant, très paternel et qui passe même à l'archevêché pour un esprit fort, un peu dangereux. Ses boutades font la joie des presbytères, et il les appuie d'un regard qu'il voudrait vif et que je trouve au fond si usé, si las, qu'il me donne envie de pleurer. (p. 1)

The archiprêtre de Bailloeil is seen to be totally out of touch with contemporary problems, concerned more with his appearance than with his effectiveness: 'un charmant vieil homme (qui) a gardé les innocentes petites manies de l'ancien professeur de lettres et soigne sa diction comme ses mains' (p. 5).[19] And above them all is the doyen de Blangermont, not only the most senior in rank, but also the one to whom Bernanos devotes most attention. As we have already seen, he is contrasted directly with the curé de Torcy in his acceptance of bourgeois society, and he supports his concern for the well-being of the Church's body rather than its soul, with the authority of the scriptures: 'Le droit de propriété n'est-il pas inscrit dans l'Evangile?' (p. 82). The only exception among these minor clerical figures is Motte-Beuvron, who in his uprightness and through his sense of the danger of mediocrity and his dislike of the 'nobles d'aujourd'hui' (pp. 228,9) is linked albeit remotely with Torcy. Like Menou-Segrais in *Sous le soleil de Satan*, who sensed Donissan's potential greatness, he also has a rather distant understanding of the young curé: 'ces gens ne haïssent pas votre simplicité, ils s'en défendent, elle est comme une espèce de feu qui les brûle' (p. 228). His role is minimal, however, and it is the magnificent Torcy who provides the outstanding contrast to the mediocre priests and who plays such an important role in relation to the curé.

Torcy, who appears on six occasions and who occupies nearly one-fifth of the book, has rightly been the centre of much critical attention. He is remarkable for his faith, his vigour and equilibrium; he is 'full of

---

[19] It is interesting to recall that Monsieur Ouine is an 'ancien professeur de langues'.

enthusiasm for social reform' and 'condemns the abuses of modern industrial society',[20] but, as the majority of critics have indicated, he belongs essentially to another age and for this reason, argue Estève and Hebblethwaite, he is not fully able to understand the problems of the modern world.[21]

Unlike the comte, whom he despises for being representative of the modern aristocracy founded on wealth, Torcy belongs to a long established and robust family which gives him the air of confidence and experience that his young colleague so much admires:

> C'est un bon prêtre, très ponctuel, que je trouve, ordinairement un peu terre à terre, un fils de paysans riches qui sait le prix de l'argent et qui m'en impose beaucoup par son expérience mondaine. (p. 9)

He also envies 'sa santé, son courage, son équilibre' (p. 10), all of which contrast directly with his own frail physical condition. Unlike the young priest, who is unable to care for himself adequately and whose domestic affairs are never better than disorganized, Torcy enjoys the good things of life. He owns a car (p. 112), he enjoys his pipe and his rooms have a splendour that the curé records with awe:

> Je ne connais pas grand'chose au mobilier, mais sa chambre m'a paru magnifique: un lit d'acajou massif, une armoire à trois portes, très sculptée, des fauteuils recouverts de peluche et sur la cheminée une énorme Jeanne d'Arc en bronze. (p. 18)

Torcy's role goes far beyond such points of comparison, however; indeed he is doubly important, first because he elaborates on a number of theories and even ideals which Bernanos expresses elsewhere in his non-imaginative writing, and second because of his relationship with the young curé.

Although we are told that Torcy belongs to the generation of Leo XIII's pontificate,[22] renowned above all for its policy of *Ralliement* (of which Bernanos disapproved), his continual references to the Middle

[20] O'Sharkey, Edition, p. 42.

[21] Estève, *Bernanos*, p. 108; Edition, p. 271. Hebblethwaite, p. 109. Lea Moch's reference p. 103 to Torcy as 'le plus parfait des prêtres de Bernanos' is a rather superficial view.

[22] *Journal d'un curé de campagne*, p. 72: 'j'ai passé pour un socialiste et les paysans bien pensants m'ont fait envoyer en disgrâce à Montreuil'.

Ages make him appear to be much more of an anachronism. In this way Bernanos is able to translate Torcy's sense of social responsibility into the terms of an era and of a system for which he nostalgically longed:

> De mon temps on formait des hommes d'église— ... oui, des hommes d'église, prenez le mot comme vous voudrez, des chefs de paroisses, des maîtres, quoi, des hommes de gouvernement. (p. 11)

In modern society the church has compromised its position of natural authority by seeking material benefit and comfort and is no longer the social force it should be. Torcy is as bitterly critical of those who expect to understand the role of the Church from attending a half-hour mass on Sundays as he is of the monks and recluses who opt out of active responsibility without being charged to do so by God. Above all he is scornful of modern training methods for the priesthood.

> Maintenant les séminaires nous envoient des enfants de chœur, des petits va-nu-pieds qui s'imaginent travailler plus que personne parce qu'ils ne viennent à bout de rien. Ça pleurniche au lieu de commander. (p. 11)

It is the need to command, to lead the struggle against evil and to revitalize society with Christian principles that underlines his entire philosophy. Like Bernanos he recognizes that evil is not something to be conquered at will. His story of the *sacristaine épatante* who fought in vain to remove all traces of dirt from his parish and even his church is a tale after the style of the Old Testament:

> Surtout, ça n'a pas été de combattre la saleté, bien sûr, mais d'avoir voulu l'anéantir, comme si c'était possible. Une paroisse, c'est sale, forcément. Une chrétienté, c'est encore plus sale. (p. 13)

Nonetheless the lesson is clear. The first duty of a priest should be to recognize the dominion of evil, to struggle against it and burn it out (p. 66), even though this necessitates isolation and demands sacrifice:

> Un vrai prêtre n'est jamais aimé, retiens ça. Et veux-tu que je te dise? L'Eglise s'en moque que vous soyez aimés, mon garçon. Soyez d'abord respectés, obéis. L'Eglise a besoin d'ordre. Faites de l'ordre en pensant que le désordre va l'emporter encore le lendemain parce qu'il est justement dans l'ordre, hélas! que la nuit fiche en l'air votre travail de la veille—la nuit appartient au diable. (p. 14)

Torcy looks in particular to Joan of Arc and to the Virgin Mary as the perfect incarnation of this attitude and in doing so significantly endows them with poverty and childlike characteristics. Saint Joan clearly represents his (and Olivier's) ideal of the militant Christian warrior, but it is not so much her warlike spirit that he admires as her belief in the rightness of what she is doing and in her trust. Similarly the Virgin Mary is portrayed in a key passage not simply as the mother of the Catholic church, but also as its daughter:

> Elle est notre mère, c'est entendu. Elle est la mère du genre humain, la nouvelle Eve. Mais elle est aussi sa fille. L'ancien monde, le douloureux monde, le monde d'avant la grâce l'a bercée longtemps sur son cœur désolé—des siècles et des siècles—dans l'attente obscure, incompréhensible d'une *virgo genitrix* . . . Des siècles et des siècles, il a protégé de ses vieilles mains chargées de crimes, ses lourdes mains, la petite fille merveilleuse dont il ne savait même pas le nom. Une petite fille, cette reine des Anges! Et elle l'est restée, ne l'oublie pas! Le moyen âge avait bien compris ça, le moyen âge a compris tout. (p. 256)

In this way the theme of faith that underpins the whole of Bernanos' work is introduced, for we are led back to the analogy of the child's dependence on its parent:

> C'est du sentiment de sa propre impuissance que l'enfant tire humblement le principe même de sa joie. Il s'en rapporte à sa mère. (p. 23)

> . . . l'Eglise a été chargée par le bon Dieu de maintenir dans le monde cet esprit d'enfance, cette ingénuité, cette fraîcheur. (pp. 24,5)

If Torcy's outstanding qualities are vigour and confidence the curé's are uncertainty, frailty and self-effacement. He is fittingly unaware of his real vocation and sees himself 'simply as an instrument used by God'.[23] As we have already noted,[24] Bernanos chooses to portray those persons selected by God for sainthood as being in some way physically weak or socially inferior. The curé d'Ambricourt is no exception; he is classless, his ancestors originally of peasant stock having left the land for the seemingly affluent life of the town (p. 41). This sense of inadequacy is accentuated by his present failure in his parochial duties, but what is so

---

[23] O'Sharkey, *Dublin Review*, p. 190.    [24] See above, pp. 13, 4.

important is not their absence or infrequent mention as his general inability to communicate. He is a poor planner of his activities, of which even the most simple seem to elude him (p. 39 and p. 108); like Donissan or Chevance before him, he is a social misfit, and he embarrasses himself and others by prolonging his visits and never knowing how to leave gracefully; he has no business sense and is easily tricked by the local shopkeepers; he is unable to care for himself properly:

Je suis chaque jour plus frappé de mon ignorance des détails les plus élémentaires de la vie pratique, que tout le monde semble connaître sans les avoir appris, par une espèce d'intuition. (p. 40)

It is typical, if unfortunate, that when the deputy mayor visits him he should be found peeling his potatoes; at once he is on the defensive: 'je me sentais ridicule' (p. 26). His shyness becomes obsessive (p. 277), he is 'paralysé par la timidité' (p. 335), and even the young children of the parish, led by Séraphita, torment him.

Physical suffering only adds to his misery. Too frail to be considered for military service (p. 42) he unwittingly aggravates his 'horribles maux d'estomac' (p. 37) by his symbolic diet of bread and wine. A sense of total abandonment and spiritual despair soon follows: 'J'étais si épuisé ce matin que j'aurais donné je ne sais quoi pour une parole humaine de compassion, de tendresse' (p. 111); 'Ma solitude est parfaite, et je la hais' (p. 132). Like Blanche de la Force in the *Dialogue des Carmélites* he loses all support and is left to undergo the various trials of his faith alone. While Torcy may in a physical sense dominate much of the action and voice a number of Bernanos' favourite themes, he is, as we have seen, both an idealist and an anachronism, and for this reason, while he may be important as the curé's spiritual guide and adviser, such a role must be limited. We should note in particular, for example, that while it is the curé who goes to visit him in the first of the episodes in which he appears (p. 9), it is he who in the last comes to the curé and by asking him for his blessing acknowledges his spiritual superiority (p. 260). In the final analysis, therefore, it is the curé who gains in stature and when Torcy leaves him for the last time we have the impression that he too has finally succumbed to the physical demands made of him by the struggle against evil: 'pour la première fois, je ne l'ai pas vu redresser sa haute taille, il marchait tout courbé' (p. 260). The lesson of strength through faith that Bernanos wishes to transmit to his readers is left to be finally and fully exemplified by the curé.

## (c) Style [25]

In a study of this kind a number of observations have inevitably been made already that could be included in an analysis of the style—the use of the first person narrative, the overall structure of the book and the balancing of episodes, the characterization and so on. In addition to such dominant features as these, however, we have less obtrusive but no less effective details in Bernanos' choice of words and images. Indeed it is these above all which give his work its final unmistakable stamp, and which in a number of key episodes draw all other aspects together into a complex whole.

Already Etienne-Alain Hubert, in his article 'L'expression romanesque du surnatural dans le *Journal d'un curé de campagne*', has made an important contribution to a study of the style of the book. As the title suggests this article relates Bernanos' descriptive method to the spiritual significance that he wishes the book to carry. Inevitably a certain amount of what Hubert has to say is standard—the oneiric quality of much of the book; the contrast drawn between darkness and light; the regular appearance of certain characteristic features, such as rain and mud, which reflect the tone of the book as a whole. His originality, however, lies in his consideration of the physical descriptions of the characters. While the diary form enables Bernanos to avoid the necessity of having to describe his characters fully, Hubert shows that he has nonetheless emphasized those features which are revelatory of their spiritual condition. Eyes and hands are particularly important. Compare for example the tired eyes of the curé de Norenfontes (p. 1) with the 'yeux si pâles (qui) souriaient en me regardant' (p. 286) of Olivier, or Dufréty's hands 'toujours tachées d'encre, et si pâles' (p. 44) with those of Torcy: 'Brusquement, il m'a pris ma main dans la sienne, une main enflée par le diabète, mais qui serre tout de suite sans tâtonner, dure, impérieuse' (pp. 15, 16). Hubert goes on to discuss the imagery used by Bernanos in the *Journal d'un curé de campagne* indicating that there are three principal types which are also characteristic of his work in general: the first relating to the animal world;[26] the second involving the idea of suffocation and contamination

[25] The most complete study of Bernanos' style to date is Blumenthal's book *The Poetic Imagination of Georges Bernanos*.

[26] There is a useful check-list of these in Albert Béguin's 'Notes sur le "Bestiaire" du *Journal d'un curé de campagne*', *Etudes bernanosiennes*, No. 2, pp. 123–5.

conveyed through the references to the fine rain, mud, dust and disease; and the third, which extends these into the idea of hidden corruption and superficiality basic to the whole tone of the book:[27]

> Beaucoup d'hommes n'engagent jamais leur être, leur sincérité profonde. Ils vivent à la surface d'eux-mêmes, et le sol humain est si riche que cette mince couche superficielle suffit pour une maigre moisson, qui donne l'illusion d'une véritable destinée. (p. 135)

In addition, while a proper appreciation of any of Bernanos' work depends on our understanding of his basic ideas about religion and society, we must also be aware of the way in which these ideas are translated into certain images and motifs. It is essential for example that we understand the importance that childhood has for Bernanos if we are to grasp fully the significance of the curé's meeting with Olivier or his thoughts at the time of Delbende's death. Similarly in the last section of the book when the curé goes to Lille we are constantly reminded of his childhood, whether it be by the references to Madame Duplouy's *estaminet*, by the doll in Laville's house or simply by his personal reflections. Other motifs which appear regularly and which are associated with particular major themes are day and night, open and closed windows and the road which stretches before Olivier's motorcycle. In a more detailed fashion individual words—*froid, clair, désespoir, amour, puissant, pauvre*, for example—are equally dependent on a precise definition if the way in which they are integrated into the text is to be fully recognized.

By this choice of imagery and vocabulary it may be argued that Bernanos is following the principle adopted by such people as Flaubert and Gide, for whom such fusion of style and theme was the hallmark of successful writing. It is also true that any regular pattern of images, especially in a work where so much has to be gleaned intuitively by the reader, opens the way to the possible charge of simplification. In *Les Anges noirs*, for example, the image of a rats' nest is basic to Mauriac's description of Liogeats and its occupants, and consequently prepares our emotional reactions. Similarly in the *Journal d'un curé de campagne*; Chantal is 'une petite bête de proie' (p. 189); Séraphita a 'petite bête farouche' (p. 280); divine Grace is referred to traditionally as water (p. 208); Satan as a 'bête ravisseuse' (p. 177), and so on. Such an accusation would only stand, however, if this system were obvious or carried

[27] Cf. Debluë, p. 69.

to excess; used with care, as in these two novels, it can be effective and also indicative of the author's close control of his material.

A further example of Bernanos' control in the *Journal d'un curé de campagne*, and one which at best has only been mentioned by his critics, is his manipulation of the language used. Like the physical features to which Hubert draws our attention it too is suited to individual characters and helps to fix them firmly in Bernanos' pattern of things. Not surprisingly perhaps the most noticeable of all is Torcy, whose vocabulary, like his personality, is colourful and full of vigour. Like the second Prieure in the *Dialogue des Carmélites*, his good sense enables him to translate abstract theological concepts into vivid images and everyday language: the seven deadly sins are described as wolves in burning paraffin (p. 73), he compares saints with musicians (p. 17) and monks with flowers (p. 15), while the word of God himself is a *dépuratif* (p. 114). He also employs local words and popular expressions—*vassingue* (p. 12), *caboche* (p. 22), *gribouille* (p. 73), *la bouche en machin de poule* (p. 66), for example. In this he is followed by Delbende who frequently expresses his forthright views in short compact sentences and clauses, and who is equally uninhibited in his choice of words—*foutre* (p. 103); *bougre* (p. 105); *ils me carottent* (p. 107). This link between character and language is traceable elsewhere. Dufréty's pretentiousness and continual need for self-justification are reflected in the way in which the subordinate clauses in his letters and conversation break into the main clauses of the sentences and hence fragment the ideas which they contain.[28] His mistress possesses the characteristics of working class speech, using *que* to avoid inversion of the subject and verb, and frequently omitting *c'est* and *il est*. Madame Dumouchel and Arsène are likewise stamped socially by what they say— the one slovenly, the other slow and ponderous. While such control of language is directly relevant to the range of social types which Bernanos portrays and to the ideas that they are required to voice, it also relieves the monotony of the curé's style. Once again we are confronted with Bernanos' concern for the artistic values of his book.

As Michel Estève has rightly observed, the curé's speech is often typified by banality, particularly in its choice of adjective (*bon, pauvre, fine* etc.).[29] What he fails to point out, however, is that just as Torcy's language is that of a Christian *soldier*, so the curé's is, in this respect at least, that of a child, and that in this way Bernanos is subtly drawing our attention to what he considers to be the most precious of all possessions.

[28] See, for example, p. 93 or the closing letter.    [29] Edition, p. 276.

There are, however, two further features that characterize the priest's diary. The first of these is an abundance of images that occur in passages other than those dominated by Torcy—the curé is indeed, as the doyen de Blangermont remarks, a poet. The second is the way in which he characteristically underestimates his role both by continually questioning his actions and also through his frequent use of the adverb *naturellement*: 'J'avais pensé donner la présidence à Sulpice Mitonnet, mais ses camarades semblent le tenir un peu à l'écart. Je n'ai pas cru devoir insister, *naturellement*' (p. 112).[30]

As with so many studies devoted to an author's style, however, such features as these, taken out of context, afford an inadequate and incomplete picture only. For their effectiveness to be fully appreciated we need to examine them in action, and in the comtesse scene in the *Journal d'un curé de campagne* we have one of the most balanced and successful examples of Bernanos' writing.[31]

On the pretext of having to settle with the comtesse the details of the service periodically held for her dead relatives, the curé arrives at the chateau unexpectedly and in a state of considerable mental and physical agitation. At once, in contrast, our attention is drawn to the peaceful surroundings outside: 'je me suis arrêté longtemps pour regarder le vieux jardinier Clovis fagotant du bois mort comme à l'ordinaire' (p. 181). For a moment the curé finds comfort in his example, but once across the threshold his nervous tension returns, and the peaceful scene he has just witnessed is forgotten: 'J'ai voulu compter les tasses, les chiffres se brouillaient dans ma tête' (p. 182), and so confused is he that he fails to notice the chair which the comtesse pushes towards him. Finally he brings himself to address her. In the brief silence that follows the curé is overwhelmed by a feeling of total inadequacy which dominates him particularly during the early part of the scene, but which also forms a protective shell around him against the comtesse's attacks. At once as though suspicious of his intrusion she is the aggressor, aiming to undermine what little confidence he might have, but he remains insensitive: 'j'étais bien incapable à cette minute de ressentir aucune offense' (p. 183). Once engaged in conversation, however, the curé's eloquence grows and with it his self assurance, but his conventional and wooden remarks—

[30] My italics. See also, for example, pp. 45, 64, 96, 216, 229.

[31] A fuller version of this analysis is to be found in my article, 'The *comtesse* episode in the *Journal d'un curé de campagne*', *French Review*, Vol. 42, No. 5, pp. 673–82.

'L'Église est à tout le monde, madame' (p. 184)—spark off a reaction which he can hardly have expected; apparently he has struck at the heart of something which for the comtesse is much more serious. Her reluctant, even bored, attention—'elle m'a regardé plusieurs fois à la dérobée, en soupirant' (p. 184)—becomes open, unconcealed hostility: 'Elle m'a regardé de nouveau, cette fois en face. Les yeux semblaient sourire encore, tandis que le bas de sa figure marquait la surprise, la méfiance, un entêtement inexprimable' (p. 184). At the same time our attention is taken from the clash of wills that is already beginning to develop, and sharply directed instead to the material setting of the scene. Before we had noticed the cups, chair, fire and poker, mentioned simply in order to ground the scene in reality; now Bernanos inserts, violently, three sentences which emphasize the curé's desperate isolation:

> Les bûches sifflaient dans l'âtre. Par la fenêtre ouverte, à travers les rideaux de linon, on voyait l'immense pelouse fermée par la muraille de pins, sous un ciel taciturne. C'était comme un étang d'eau croupissante. (p. 184)

The open window, which reappears on two later occasions during this scene and is frequently in Bernanos' work a symbol of hope and infinite love, here looks out on the oppressive elements of darkness. The alliterative play on 's', particularly in 'Les bûches sifflaient' and 'sous un ciel taciturne', together with the final image of a stagnant swamp all contribute to the impression of violence and latent evil. The comtesse also changes: 'L'être que j'avais devant moi ne ressemblait guère . . . à celui que j'avais imaginé' (p. 185) and her sudden outburst of laughter (p. 185)—in Bernanos' work a common sign of demonic possession— reminds us of her own daughter earlier in the novel (pp. 164,5), Mouchette in Sous le soleil de Satan or Cénabre in L'Imposture. The scene has passed through its initial phase. Believing that he is primarily concerned with an issue involving a mother and her daughter, the curé has unwittingly released a much deeper anguish in the comtesse's soul. The increase in tempo which this produces is emphasized by the sudden inclusion of the material setting and is finally caught in the comtesse's physical suffering. At this point, however, the rhythm begins to relax and the comtesse, as though aware that she has been brought to the brink of a full confession, attempts to bring their conversation back to Chantal. For a moment at least the full climactic fury that is to be released later has been allayed; Bernanos has also sustained the tension.

The following two pages act as a brief interlude in this struggle between the young priest's charity and the comtesse's apparent indifference, but his immense sympathy together with his capacity to suffer vicariously seems to urge the comtesse paradoxically both to brave him and to confess. Again an image of decay and corruption heralds a renewed quickening of pace: 'Un prêtre est comme un médecin, il ne doit pas avoir peur des plaies, du pus, de la sanie. Toutes les plaies de l'âme suppurent, madame' (p. 186). A second crisis is imminent: 'Elle semblait redouter que je la quittasse et en même temps lutter contre l'envie de tout dire, de livrer son pauvre secret.' In the second phase of the scene further material is brought to the curé's attention; the comtesse confesses to the jealousy which has dominated her relationship with Chantal, but once more breaks off, uncertain of where her frenzied impetuosity has led her. The pattern of the preceding pages begins to re-emerge and predictably the curé notices a physical change which comes over her:

> Quoi! était-ce la même dame, si réservée, si douce qu'à ma première visite au château, j'avais vue blottie au fond de sa grande bergère, son visage pensif, sous la dentelle noire? . . . Sa voix même était si changée que j'avais peine à la reconnaître, elle devenait criarde, traînait sur les dernières syllabes. (p. 188)

This time, however, Bernanos allows the process to continue. The image of emergent evil reappears as this spiritual combat is seen as an actual physical confrontation (p. 189) and as before the outside world is introduced, this time in the form of lashing rain, to focus our attention even more sharply on the isolated nature of the struggle. The pattern of the first phase has been perfectly repeated. Similarly, as one upward movement suggesting an imminent crisis has followed another, so too does the tension now relax:

> Je me souviens aussi du vieux Clovis qui, sa besogne faite, s'essuyait les mains à son tablier bleu. On entendait, de l'autre côté du vestibule, un bruit de verres choqués, de vaisselle remuée. Tout était calme, facile, familier. (p. 189)

But the calm is short-lived. Now for the first time the comtesse mentions her infant son, and from this point the rhythm of the scene steadily accelerates. As the curé observes, 'Elle avait l'air de glisser sur une pente' (p. 189).

With the death of her son the comtesse had become isolated within her

D

family, her husband and Chantal—'Si exactement faits l'un pour l'autre' (p. 190)—sharing a life of which she was allowed no part. Her pathetic pride at having endured the torment of this exclusion, in addition to her husband's infidelities, invokes the priest's pity, and the scene moves rapidly to a repetition of the by now familiar pattern, albeit this time without the accompaniment of external features: an apparently unprovoked desire to confess—'vous êtes un rusé petit prêtre' (p. 191)—and the usual mental and physical disturbance reflected this time not only in the comtesse's 'regard égaré' and her 'voix sifflante' (p. 191), but also in her uncontrollable destruction of the fan (p. 192). It is at this point that the difference between the curé's concern and the comtesse's as yet unconfessed plight meet in ironic contrast. For the curé the visit to the chateau has been made in an attempt to reconcile the comtesse with her daughter; for him, her anxiety appears to stem from a long nourished hatred of Chantal and no more. His priestly concern for her soul prompts him to express his fear that she will die before the matter is settled, but it is also so intense that he has a vision of her dead. She too suddenly becomes aware of his fears and her reaction again suggests that for her the matter is much more deep-rooted and unrevealed. These two attitudes to the same vision accelerate the pace of the scene even more through a number of digressions until the comtesse is finally forced to declare the true cause of her torment. Her bitterness over Chantal's relationship with her father builds up to the same hysterical pitch reached before. This time, however, it is more acute and more sustained, but as the climax of the scene draws closer so too does the possibility of the sudden influx of grace. Evil is now distilled within this single room; outside, the gardens and trees are no longer the hostile elements they were only minutes before: 'A travers les vitres trempées de pluie, je voyais le parc, si noble, si calme, les courbes majestueuses des pelouses, les vieux arbres solennels' (p. 194).

The temporary digression, which is now introduced, involving the notion of Christian example and leadership, and recalling the idealistic visions of the curé de Torcy, is necessary both to change the subject of their conversation from Chantal to the baby, and also to suspend the climax once again: 'Je sentais que mes dernières paroles lui avaient donné le temps de se reprendre' (p. 197). The curé prepares to leave, but the comtesse makes a final effort to retain him and, as she does, he notices 'dans ses yeux une inquiétude incompréhensible' (p. 198). At last against her will she finds herself admitting that she fears for Chantal's life, an admission which has been forced from her quite simply by the curé's presence and which is the inevitable outcome of the scene so far. Yet this is only part of the eventual climax. Her anguish is not simply the result of a clash of equally unbending prides, as the curé still imagines it to be, and his sudden loss of patience snaps her resistance at last uncovering its real source; her quarrel is not with Chantal but with God.

Having now laid bare the real cause of the comtesse's anguish, Bernanos moves into the key passage not only of the scene, but of the novel as a whole—his discussion of hell. Through her refusal to accept God's will and to trust in His love, believing instead that she could create an existence of her own with the memory of her dead son, the comtesse is already placing herself on the threshold of hell, a state which neither she nor any mortal can truly conceive: 'On juge l'enfer d'après les maximes de ce monde et l'enfer n'est pas de ce monde' (p. 200). Real Hell is to be found in complete and utter isolation: 'L'erreur commune à tous est d'attribuer à ces créatures abandonnées quelque chose de nous, de notre perpétuelle mobilité alors qu'elles sont hors du temps, hors du mouvement, fixées pour toujours' (p. 201). Creatures in this state have not only lost contact with God but also with one another: 'Le malheur, l'inconcevable malheur de ces pierres embrasées qui furent des hommes, c'est qu'elles n'ont plus rien à partager' (p. 201). For the comtesse, however, as for all mankind, salvation is still possible, but it necessitates in her case an unquestioning acceptance of her son's death. As a priest the curé's duty is to convince her of this, but his attempts meet at first with violent revolt: 'cette fois j'ai vu la révolte, la vraie révolte, éclater sur un visage humain' (p. 205). But it is momentary only. He has brought her face to face with God, with her own decision, and her physical surrender—'Elle s'est laissée tomber dans son fauteuil, la tête entre ses mains' (p. 207)—marks the beginning of her eventual complete submission, though it is not achieved without a struggle. The climax of the scene has at last been reached and Bernanos prolongs it through another four pages. Unlike the abbé Donissan, whose one mistake was to challenge God on His own terms, the curé must persuade the comtesse of the need to submit: 'on ne marchande pas avec le bon Dieu, il faut se rendre à lui, sans condition' (p. 208). Clearly for the comtesse to accept his word, grace must effect a change within her, but this is no sudden conversion. The tension created by the problem is detailed for us not in the vague terms of some unseen supernatural event, but in the very *human* suffering which she is obliged to undergo. Her son's last minutes alive are recalled with the genuine anguish of a normal mother and she suffers physically: 'Elle s'est mise à

trembler comme une feuille' (p. 209). The curé's task is to persuade her
of God's overwhelming love, of His power and willingness to assume all
human misery and suffering. In addition the external features of the scene
once again serve as clues in aiding us to understand the supernatural
process which is at work, but while before they had been hostile, now, as
we have already noticed, they are at peace.

It is at this point, however, that the scene takes a violent and ironical
turn. The comtesse imagines that her own unyielding hate can only be
truly redeemed by absolute sacrifice, and her act of throwing the locket
containing a curl of her son's hair into the fire indicates how literally and
despairingly she interprets the curé's words: 'Donnez votre orgueil avec
le reste, donnez tout' (p. 211), but whatever the subsequent results of this
act may be in the rest of the novel, the spell that has bound the comtesse
since her son's death has at last been broken, and peace settles on the room
for the first time since the curé set foot in it a short while earlier: 'nous
étions rentrés si doucement dans la vie de chaque jour que le témoin le
plus attentif n'eût rien surpris de ce secret, qui déjà ne nous appartenait
plus' (p. 212). The substitution of good for evil has been achieved without
any recourse whatsoever to supernatural or unexplained phenomena. As
she dresses his burns the comtesse becomes, ironically, a mother figure, a
reflection not only of her true nature but an allusion as well to the mother
of the Catholic Church, the Virgin Mary. Yet still the process is incomplete. With his parting words the curé is overcome by a feeling of sadness
which both echoes his mental and physical disarray on his arrival at the
chateau, and also looks forward to the comtesse's death which occurs a
few hours later.

He leaves the chateau for the neighbouring village of Dombasle. He is
physically exhausted, emptied by the struggle he has had to endure, but
at the same time filled with a sense of indefinable achievement, 'une joie
sans visage'. On his return a chance meeting with Clovis recalling the
opening scene of the whole episode gives it formal shape, and the locket
with its symbolically broken chain which the gardener brings from the
comtesse, together with her letter with its reference to the curé as a
child, imposes a thematic unity.

Considered in its entirety this episode has a unity and tension created
by the inclusion of certain standard themes—childhood, love, hell, for
example—which are often all but lost beneath the frenzy of refusal and
revolt which verges at times on hysteria and insanity. Only an awareness
of the comtesse's true dilemma and also of her sense of guilt enables us to

detect a meaningful structure in the otherwise apparently illogical sequence of her speeches. Similarly we must suspect that the comtesse's anguish stems from something greater than a simple clash of unbending wills, if we are to appreciate to the full the sudden bursts of confession followed by retractions and changes of subject. The typical Bernanos images are there—the stagnant swamp and the suppurating sores—so too are individual words and phrases: *pourri* (p. 196); *abcès* (p. 199); *ver dans le fruit* (p. 204). Most impressive of all, however, is the way in which Bernanos also manipulates the actual formal structure of the episode, so that the surging rhythm that is its characteristic, continually hints at the pent up fury that it contains but never, until the final climax, actually allows it to be released.

In 1939 Bernanos remarked that 'La Poésie n'est rien si elle n'est le chant de notre misère'[32] and indeed the whole of the comtesse episode may be read as an extended prose poem. An introductory section (pp. 181,2) is followed by a series of episodes each one more intense and compelling than its predecessor. The first spans three pages (pp. 182–5) and is followed by a break of some length (pp. 186,7); the second, which is more extended (pp. 187–92), is rapidly followed by the third (pp. 192–7), highlighted by the vision the curé has of the dead comtesse and containing the short digression on Christian example and responsibility. This, in turn, is separated by a single page from the fourth part of this underlying rhythmic pattern (pp. 198–206) which crystallizes the comtesse's anguish and introduces the central theme of God's love. Here the rapid explosive movement of the earlier passages changes to a controlled preparation of the ultimate climax (pp. 206–11) as the comtesse deliberates on the curé's words and as grace slowly destroys her former proud self-sufficiency. When it eventually arrives the climax is, by comparison, rapid and almost brutal, five sentences alone describing her supreme sacrifice (pp. 211,12). The final pages, which contain the curé's departure from the chateau and his return to the village later the same evening, are infused with an air of peace, as is the comtesse's death, which, noted in a single line, closes the episode.

Such is the overall pattern of this central section of the novel, which owes its internal tension to certain recurring images and words and to standard themes. In addition the unwitting misrepresentation of the central issue by both the curé and the comtesse, together with the power which the curé has to force her ultimately to confess in spite of herself,

[32] *Le Crépuscule des vieux*, p. 124.

creates an undertone of ironic suspense. More significantly the struggle between them is one of humility and innocence against intellectual pride; it echoes the clash between Chevance's simple faith and Cénabre's spiritless intellectual inquiry and hagiology in *L'Imposture*. Cénabre eventually dies having rediscovered his faith; so does the comtesse. And, in doing so, each of them illustrates the aim which Bernanos set himself as early as 1905:

> nous ne pouvons valoir quelque chose que par le sacrifice et l'oubli total de soi au profit de Dieu et de sa cause, et que le meilleur moyen d'arriver au mépris de la mort est l'offrande de la vie et de la mort.[33]

The ideas that Bernanos wishes his readers to grasp have been given their perfect form and style of expression. While in its beauty and power this scene is exceptional, the *Journal d'un curé de campagne* possesses thematic and stylistic unity that, with the possible exception of the *Nouvelle Histoire de Mouchette*, is absent from any of his other novels.

[33] Letter to the abbé Lagrange quoted in *Œuvres romanesques*, pp. 1729,30.

# 5. Conclusion

When in 1926 Bernanos remarked in an interview with Frédéric Lefèvre 'Je n'aurais pas voulu *mourir sans témoigner*',[1] he stated a principle that was to stand for all his subsequent work and which placed it firmly in the ranks of committed literature. At once the problem common to all such work arises, namely that of conveying a certain belief or interpretation of events without at the same time creating the impression that he is being in any way didactic or edifying. We have already noted that Bernanos was aware of this,[2] but his attempts to avoid it or to find a solution were not always successful. *La Joie* in particular is a good example of how his preoccupation with religious faith regulates events to such an extent that the work's literary values are in danger of being entirely destroyed. In the *Journal d'un curé de campagne*, however, the same interpretation of religious faith is incorporated in such a way that at no time does it appear out of place. We have every right to disagree with the young curé's faith, but as a personal experience it must be allowed to stand unchallenged as a feature of his life as it is recorded through his diary. As long as his actions remain independent of any supernatural intervention we are not in a position to accuse Bernanos of having introduced material that falls outside the range of our normal experience. Certainly, to use Ernest Beaumont's words, the curé 'se conforme ... à la vie christique, il se laisse pénétrer par le Christ',[3] but such final sublimation is not achieved at the expense of human interest, and it is in this that the book's success lies. The curé is required to undergo a series of tests (*épreuves*) from which he emerges triumphant, but at no time does he receive any *unexplained* divine assistance. Clearly he does benefit from it, but, while his moments of vision and intuition are intended to be rewards for his faith, they can also be seen to have been induced by the *human* situations in which they occur, and it is through these that Bernanos succeeds both in conveying his message and in creating the book's dramatic tension.

The early part of the book and in particular the opening section is, we

---

[1] *Le Crépuscule des vieux*, p. 67.   [2] See above, p. 14.
[3] *Etudes bernanosiennes*, Vol. 3/4, pp. 90,1.

recall, devoted mainly to the creation of context and atmosphere. The curé's suffering is underlined and his willingness to die on behalf of his parish is deliberately recorded: ('ma première et dernière paroisse peut-être, car je souhaiterais d'y mourir' (p. 35)); and soon after this, the important description of Ambricourt from a nearby hill, immediately followed by the analogy with Calvary and Christ's Crucifixion, leaves us in no doubt of Bernanos' intention:

> Au haut de la côte, qu'il pleuve ou vente, je m'asseois sur un tronc de peuplier oublié là on ne sait pourquoi depuis des hivers et qui commence à pourrir . . . je ne trouverais pas un autre observatoire d'où le village m'apparaisse ainsi tout entier comme ramassé dans le creux de la main. Je le regarde, et je n'ai jamais l'impression qu'il me regarde aussi. Je ne crois pas d'ailleurs non plus qu'il m'ignore. On dirait qu'il me tourne le dos et m'observe de biais, les yeux mi-clos, à la manière des chats.

> . . . Quoi que je fasse, lui aurais-je donné jusqu'à la dernière goutte de mon sang (et c'est vrai que parfois j'imagine qu'il m'a cloué là-haut sur une croix, qu'il me regarde au moins mourir), je ne le posséderais pas. (pp. 48,9)

From this point until the appearance of Torcy's friend Delbende the diary is largely devoted to a discussion of Christian society and values not only preparing for the role which Bernanos believes belongs to the priest, but also for Delbende, who has broken with the Church on these very grounds. For the doctor who represents the first of his major *épreuves*, the curé experiences immediate sympathy. As with the comtesse later in the book he is here confronted with an unbeliever whom it is his duty as a priest to reconcile with God. Unlike the comtesse episode, however, there is little confrontation or debate. Instead the curé's anguish arising from his sense of inadequacy not only dominates the content of the diary entries but also their form.[4] They become here much shorter and more brittle, and entire pages are destroyed for the first time (p. 133) as though he is unable to express and moreover preserve his sense of growing despair. Only with the noting of Delbende's death does this episode assume in retrospect a greater significance. Only now do we realize that the curé's anguish has been an expression of the truly priestly quality of vicarious suffering, while the appearance of childhood images in his writing indicates the conclusion that Bernanos asks us to draw.

---

[4] References to night, which in Bernanos' work traditionally accompany the workings of evil, are also numerous at this point in the diary.

Apart from his meeting with Olivier and with Dufréty's mistress immediately before his death, the curé's anguish is unrelieved for the rest of the book. He finds comfort and support solely in his faith which stands as a last defence between him and total despair. For Bernanos to retain the dramatic, human interest of the book, however, personal fulfilment alone is not enough, nor is the curé's ability to suffer vicariously, a characteristic which we can only intuit from his diary. As a priest it is also his duty to convince others of the truth of God's love, and the comtesse scene provides us with the outstanding illustration of this in the book. As with the Delbende episode Bernanos is careful in his preparation. The curé's long discussion of purity (pp. 152–7) is directly relevant to the comtesse's situation; purity, he argues, is necessary if faith is to be preserved, for its loss leads to the type of existence based on lies and self-delusion that is a certain step towards damnation:

> la pureté . . . est une des conditions mystérieuses mais évidentes,—l'expérience l'atteste—de cette connaissance surnaturelle de soi-même, de soi-même en Dieu, qui s'appelle la foi. L'impureté ne détruit pas cette connaissance, elle en anéantit le besoin. On ne croit plus, parce qu'on ne désire plus croire. Vous ne désirez plus vous connaître. (p. 157)

These words apply directly both to the comtesse and to Chantal, and once again it is his duty as a priest to make them realize the emptiness of their lives, a task which he can only undertake alone with no support other than that of his faith.[5]

While the scene with Chantal is important in its own right it also prefigures that with her mother. Each possesses the same basic characteristics—the curé's sense of inferiority which is gradually transformed into one of dominance; his powers of vision and intuition induced by his intense sense of pity and powers of concentration; his physical suffering. In particular the second of the two scenes, which occurs precisely at the middle of the book and marks the climax to its dramatic movement, is perhaps the most successful enactment of Bernanos' perpetual theme of the clash between good and evil. The curé's account of the scene differs from our interpretation of it, but any doubt we may have of his true stature is dispelled when he significantly slips the comtesse's letter into his copy of the Imitation (p. 215). From this point he becomes increasingly Christlike, though it is not until he has resisted the ultimate temptation of

[5] Torcy's absence is recorded on p. 159; he only returns on p. 245.

suicide that he is rewarded by the revelation through Torcy of his true vocation (p. 248). Having advanced to this state the diary now becomes less of an account of the curé's relationship with other people and more one of his mental, spiritual and physical state. Olivier and Laville, for example, though important in themselves,[6] are no less so for the reactions and reflections which they inspire in the curé. In this way, just as Olivier shares Torcy's affection for the militant Christianity of the Middle Ages and hence helps to illustrate one of Bernanos' key themes, he is also necessary as a passive element in the account of the curé's spiritual development.

In addition to this more intense focusing on the curé's personal reflections the analogies with Christ also become more noticeable. Throughout the book his staple diet of bread and wine acts as a constant reminder of his essential role; so too do more minor incidents or remarks. Now this sense of general identification is made sharper in particular by the use Bernanos makes of the Way of the Cross in the scene in which the curé is discovered by Séraphita and in which he also has a vision of the Virgin Mary (pp. 263–7); it is also more apparent in the third section of the book as he approaches his death. At no point, however, does the curé become an allegorical figure of Christ and transcend the limits of reality. It is possible, for example, to explain his vision of the Virgin Mary (pp. 264–6) in purely psychological terms (in the way that some dreams can be explained) since only hours before Torcy has talked to him at length about this very subject. Similarly his immediate reaction to the news that he is going to die is a very normal one of panic, from which only his faith enables him to recover.

From this general movement of the book it becomes clear that Bernanos requires the curé to illustrate his own belief that life without God is valueless.[7] Certainly he makes no attempt to soften his view of society, nor does he pretend that the curé does not suffer. Evil remains dominant and faith is not something to be adopted or rejected at will as a short cut to comfort and peace of mind. Once accepted and held in the face of severe temptation, however, its positive value and rewards become apparent; the curé therefore is an example to be followed. It is in the choice of the diary form, however, that the *Journal d'un curé de campagne* succeeds where *La Joie* had failed. Not only has Bernanos been able to disguise a number of important features which we associate with a more conventional form of novel writing, but he has also assured himself of an

[6] See above, pp. 36,7.          [7] See above, p. 10.

unchallengeable means of expression for a personal belief. In this way whether or not we choose to accept this belief becomes irrelevant; what we must concern ourselves with are the literary merits of the book and these, as I have tried to show, are many and unquestionable.

# Biographical Note

1888      Born in Paris.
Childhood holidays spent at Fressin, Pas de Calais, frequently recalled with affection in his work. Early reading of Balzac.

1898–1906      School education in Paris, Bourges and Sainte-Marie d'Aire-sur-la-Lys. Friendship with abbé Lagrange. Early interest in Charles Maurras and the Action Française.

1906–13      Successfully follows his *licence en droit* and *licence ès lettres*.

1907      Seven short stories published in *Le Panache*.

1908      Becomes a *camelot du roi* and is deeply involved in Action Française activities.

1913–14      Editor of Royalist weekly *L'Avant-garde de Normandie*.

1914–18      War service.

1917      Marriage to Jeanne Talbert d'Arc.

1926      Publication of his first novel *Sous le soleil de Satan*. Its success encourages Bernanos to devote himself to writing and during the next four years he completes two more novels, *L'Imposture* (1926) and *La Joie* (1929).

1930–4      Begins work on *Un Mauvais Rêve*, *Monsieur Ouine* and *Un Crime*. Publishes various essays and in particular *La Grande Peur des bien-pensants* (1931).

1934–7      Lives in Majorca. *Un Crime* published in 1935. Begins work on the *Journal d'un curé de campagne* and the *Nouvelle Histoire de Mouchette*, published in 1937.

1935–6      November–February, *Journal d'un curé de campagne* serialized in the *Revue hebdomadaire*. Published in March by Plon the book is awarded the Grand Prix du Roman by the Académie Française. Its success guarantees Bernanos financial security.

1937–8      Returns to France and rewrites the *Grands cimetières sous la lune* (1938) having lost the original manuscript.

1938–45      Lives in South America. *Monsieur Ouine* completed in 1940. Writing otherwise confined to more volumes of essays and journalism. E.g. *Nous Autres Français* (1939) and *Lettre aux Anglais* (1942).

1945–8     Returns to France. Writes his last literary work, the *Dialogue des Carmélites*, published after his death in 1949. Begins a *Vie de Jésus*.

5 July. Death of Bernanos at Neuilly.

# Select Bibliography

(a) *Editions of the* Journal d'un curé de campagne

The text used for this essay is that of the first edition published by Plon, Paris, 1936.

*Bernanos: Œuvres romanesques* (Bibl. de la Pléiade), N.R.F., Paris, 1961, contains some useful introductory notes and an important collection of letters to the abbé Lagrange.

*Journal d'un curé de campagne*, Livre de Poche Université, Paris, 1964. Edited by M. Estève.

*Georges Bernanos: Journal d'un curé de campagne*, University of London Press, London, 1969 (Textes français classiques et modernes). Edited by E. O'Sharkey.

(b) *General studies of Bernanos' work*

(i) *Books*

Hans Urs von Balthasar, *Le Chrétien Bernanos*, Editions du Seuil, Paris, 1956.

Albert Béguin, *Bernanos par lui-même*, Editions du Seuil, Paris, 1954.

Michel Estève, *Bernanos*, Gallimard, Paris, 1965 (Bibliothèque idéale).

Peter Hebblethwaite, *Bernanos*, Bowes and Bowes, Cambridge and London, 1965 (Studies in Modern European Literature and Thought).

Max Milner, *Georges Bernanos*, Desclée de Brouwer, Paris, 1967.

(ii) *Articles*

*Etudes bernanosiennes*, Minard, Paris. Ten volumes (of which Nos. 3 and 4 form a double volume) have been published between 1960 and 1969.

Ernest Beaumont, 'Georges Bernanos, 1888–1948', in *The Novelist as Philosopher* (ed. J. Cruickshank), Oxford University Press, London, 1962, pp. 29–54.

(c) *Studies relevant to the* Journal d'un curé de campagne

(i) *Books*

Hans Aaraas, *A propos du Journal d'un curé de campagne: essai sur l'écrivain et le prêtre dans l'œuvre romanesque de Bernanos*, Archives des Lettres modernes, No. 70, Minard, Paris, 1966.

Yves Bridel, *L'esprit de l'enfance dans l'œuvre romanesque de Georges Bernanos*, Minard, Paris, 1966 (Chapter V).

Gerda Blumenthal, *The poetic imagination of Georges Bernanos*, John Hopkins Press, Baltimore, 1965 (Chapter VI).

Henri Dubluë, *Les romans de Georges Bernanos, ou le défi du rêve*, La Baconnière, Neuchâtel, 1965 (Chapter V).

Max Milner, *Georges Bernanos*, Desclée de Brouwer, Paris, 1967 (Chapter X).

Lea Moch, *La sainteté dans les romans de Georges Bernanos*, Société des editions 'Les Belles Lettres', Paris, 1962 (Part II).

(ii) *Articles*

*Etudes bernanosiennes*, No. 2, Winter 1961,2 contains the following articles:

Michel Estève, 'Genèse du *Journal d'un curé de campagne*', pp. 3–15.

Etienne-Alain Hubert, 'Quelques aspects de l'expression romanesque du surnaturel dans le *Journal d'un curé de campagne*', pp. 19–53.

Nicole Winter, 'Conception bernanosienne du sacerdoce à partir du *Journal d'un curé de campagne*', pp. 87–121.

Albert Béguin, 'Notes sur le "Bestiaire" du *Journal d'un curé de campagne*', pp. 123–5.

Michel Estève, 'Une présentation du *Journal d'un curé de campagne* de Georges Bernanos', *Le Français dans le monde*, No. 11, Sept. 1962, pp. 43–8.

John Flower, 'The *comtesse* episode in the *Journal d'un curé de campagne*', *French Review*, Vol. 45, No. 5, April, 1969, pp. 673–82.

Eithne O'Sharkey, 'Portraits of the Clergy in Bernanos' *Diary of a Country Priest*', *Dublin Review*, No. 504, Summer 1965, pp. 183–91.